The Shepherd's Voice

Joshua Rhoades

Published by Joshua Paul Rhoades, 2024.

While every precaution has been taken in the preparation of this book, the publisher assumes no responsibility for errors or omissions, or for damages resulting from the use of the information contained herein.

THE SHEPHERD'S VOICE

First edition. October 28, 2024.

ISBN: 979-8227586711

Written by Joshua Rhoades.

Also by Joshua Rhoades

Courage Under Fire: David's Stand On The Battlefield
Jonah's Journey: Voices Of Redemption And Lessons In Obedience
The Furnace Of Faith: 12 Principles From The Heat Of Faith
Whispers of Hope: Inspiring Stories of Men's Prayers In Scripture
Frontier Legends: The Oregon Dream
Elijah: A Beacon Of Boldness
HOOK, LINE & SAVIOUR - Faith Reflections from Fishing
Driven By Faith: Motor Racing Inspired Christian Life
30 Day Devotional - Bold and Strong- Coffee Devotions for a Courageous
Christian Walk
Authentic Christianity: The Heart of Old Time Religion
Consider The Ant - God's Tiny Preachers
Flee Fornication: The Plea For Purity
Renewed Hope- How to Find Encouragement in God
Sounding The Call - The Voice of Conviction
The Altar - Where Heaven Meets Earth
The Bible's Battlefields- Timeless Lessons from Ancient Wars
The Sacred Art of Silence - How Silence Speaks in Scripture
Under Fire- The Sanctity of the Traditional Biblical Home
Who Is on the Lord's Side? A Call to Righteousness
What Is Truth? - From Skepticism to Submission
First and Goal- Faith and Football Fundamentals
From Dugout to Devotion- Spiritual Lessons from Baseball
Par for the Course- Faith and Fairways
The Believer's Pace- Tools for Running Life's Marathon
The Immutable Fortress- Security in God's Unchanging Nature
Biblical Bravery
Deer Stands and Devotions: A Hunter's Walk with God

Jesus Knows- Our Hearts, Our Responsibility

Restoration - Setting The Bone

Spiritual 911- God's Word for Life's Emergency's

The Freedom of Forgiveness

The Jezebel Effect - Ancient Manipulations Modern Lessons

The Shout That Stopped The Saviour

The Time Machine Chronicles: Old Testament Characters

Anchored In Truth Exploring The Depths of Psalm 119

Biblical Counsel on Anger

Proverbs' Portraits The Men God Mentions

Stumbling in the Dark - The Dangers of Alcohol

Guarding the Wicket Protecting Your Faith and Game

The Champion's Faith - Wrestling and Achieving Spiritual Victory

Scriptural Commands for Modern Times Living God's Word Today Volume 1

Scriptural Commands for Modern Times Living God's Word Today Volume 2

Scriptural Commands for Modern Times Living God's Word TodayVolume3

The Greatest Gift

A Christmas Journey of Faith

Daughter Of The King: Embracing Your Identity In Christ

Determination and Dedication Building Strong Faith As A Young Man

Walking Through Walls God's Power to Part the Storms of Life

David's Song Of Deliverance Praising God Through Every Storm

From Weakness to Warrior: Gideon's Transformation

Why Did Jesus Weep?

Living For God The Call To Be A Living Sacrifice

My Mind Is In A Fog What Do I Do?

Turning The Page Written By Grace

The Calling and Greatness of John the Baptist

For Such a Time Esther's Courageous Stand

From Brokenness To Beauty Written By The Pen of Grace

The Ultimate Guide to Massive Action- From Plans to Reality

A Heart Of Conviction

Serving In The Shadows

Repentance Revealed The Road Back To God

The Chief Sinner Meets The Chief Saviour Reflections On I Timothy 1:15

Answer The Call - 31 Days of Biblical Action
The Birthmark of the Believer
Reflections on Calvary's Cross
The Kingdom Builder Paul's Bold Proclamation of Christ
The Animal Of Pride
The Reach That Restores Christ Love For The Broken
Paul- The Many Roles of a Servant of Christ
Unshakeable Faith- 31 Days of Peace in God's Word
O Come, Let Us Adore Him- A Christmas Devotional
The Shepherd's Voice

Dedication

To you, dear reader,

This book, "The Shepherd's Voice", is dedicated to you, to the unique path you're walking, and to the silent hopes and questions you carry in your heart. Whether you're here seeking comfort, strength, or just a reminder that you're not alone, know that each word in this book was written with you in mind, as if spoken directly to you. Life's journey isn't always easy; it has moments of joy but also valleys of doubt and times when we feel lost or overwhelmed. This book is here to be a guide, a source of encouragement, and a gentle reminder that, no matter where you are or what you're facing, you are not walking this path alone. The Shepherd, who knows every detail of your life and loves you deeply, is with you, speaking to you, guiding you through each step with a voice that is as steady as it is kind.

May each chapter be a touchstone of hope and a reassurance that you are seen, known, and valued. Let the Shepherd's voice bring comfort to your heart, peace to your spirit, and renewed courage to face each day. As you read, allow yourself to rest in the truth that His voice is not just a distant sound—it's a warm, familiar call that meets you where you are, in your joys and in your struggles. This voice invites you to lay down your worries, release your burdens, and find rest in a love that is unshakable. Know that you are cherished beyond measure by the One who knows you fully, the One who has walked with you through every season of life, even when you couldn't see or feel His presence.

So, as you turn these pages, may you feel a quiet, strengthening presence beside you, a voice that whispers hope and a promise of peace that no trial can take away. May this book serve as a reminder that you are infinitely loved by a Shepherd who will never leave your side, who calls you by name, and who leads you toward a life of purpose, grace, and fulfillment. Let His voice be a lamp to your feet, a light to your path, and a source of unending encouragement, today and always. You are forever held, forever loved, and forever guided by the One who will never let you go. This journey is yours, but you are never alone.

Introduction

Welcome to "The Shepherd's Voice", a journey into understanding, feeling, and following the steady, gentle guidance of Jesus Christ, our Great Shepherd. In life, we all experience times when the path seems unclear, when choices overwhelm us, and when we feel alone, uncertain, or even afraid. This book is here to remind you that you are not alone, even in the quiet or dark places. You have a Shepherd who knows you fully, who loves you deeply, and who speaks to you in ways that calm your heart, strengthen your spirit, and bring light to the road ahead. Imagine for a moment the peace and strength that come from knowing that no matter where you find yourself today, there is Someone who cares about every step you take. Jesus, the Shepherd of our souls, calls to us with a voice that is gentle yet powerful, filled with compassion and wisdom, and able to speak directly to our hearts. His voice is like a soft but steady whisper, sometimes almost hidden in the noise of life but always there, waiting for us to listen. This Shepherd doesn't lead from a distance; He is close, present, and patient. He walks with us, beside us, and sometimes even carries us when we feel we can't move forward. His voice isn't just another sound in our lives; it is the voice that knows exactly what we need, whether that's comfort in hard times, direction when we're lost, or courage to keep going when we're tired. In every chapter, you'll find stories, reflections, and insights that show the many ways the Shepherd's voice speaks to us, how it comforts us, and how it helps us grow. Whether you are familiar with faith or exploring it for the first time, this book invites you to open your heart and listen to this loving, guiding voice. It's about recognizing that the Shepherd's voice is unique – it is gentle, it does not force or demand, but it calls to us in a way that makes us want to follow, to trust, and to feel safe. You'll discover that following the Shepherd's voice isn't about knowing every answer or being perfect; it's about being willing to take one step at a time, trusting that His guidance is always good, that His wisdom is beyond what we see, and that His love for us is unchanging. This voice is one that meets us right where we are, no matter our mistakes, doubts, or fears. It calls us by name, reassuring us that we are valuable, loved, and never forgotten. As you journey through the pages of "The Shepherd's Voice", my hope is that you will feel His presence close to you, that you will recognize His care for you, and that you will find a new sense of peace, knowing that you are held and guided by a Shepherd who knows every detail of your life and walks with you through every high and low. May this book be a companion that helps you lean into the quiet moments, listen deeply, and follow with confidence, knowing that the Shepherd's voice will always lead you safely forward.

Chapter 1 - Steady Voice

The Shepherd's voice is a steady voice, one that gently guides us and provides comfort, wisdom, and reassurance when life feels confusing or overwhelming. Imagine walking along a winding path with obstacles you can't see ahead, where each step feels uncertain, and your heart is unsure of which direction to take. That is when the Shepherd's voice speaks, not loudly or forcefully, but in a calm, steady way, saying, "This is the way, walk ye in it." It's as if He's walking right behind us, offering us a quiet but strong presence that encourages us to take each step with confidence, no matter how unsure we feel. This voice doesn't rush us or push us into something we're not ready for; instead, it's patient, allowing us to move forward at a pace we can handle, reassuring us that it's okay not to know everything, not to see the entire journey ahead. The Shepherd's voice gives us just enough guidance for each moment, helping us to trust the path we're on, even if we don't have all the answers. It tells us that we don't need to fear what we can't see or worry about what's beyond our control because we're not walking alone. There's a comfort in knowing that someone who loves us deeply is watching out for us, guiding us with a voice that is filled with kindness and understanding. His voice doesn't demand perfection from us; it simply asks us to listen and to trust that He knows the way, even when we don't. This steady voice speaks to our hearts, calming our fears and helping us to focus on what truly matters, reminding us that every step we take is significant, even the small or hesitant ones. It's a voice that acknowledges our worries and our doubts, yet it provides peace that helps us to keep moving forward. When we feel lost or discouraged, the Shepherd's voice reassures us that we are not forgotten, that our journey has meaning, and that each step is part of a larger plan that He understands, even if we don't. This voice knows the way because the Shepherd has walked it before us, and He sees what we cannot. The Shepherd's voice is steady, even when everything else around us feels chaotic or uncertain. It doesn't waver or change, and it isn't dependent on how we feel or what we think. His voice remains a constant source of direction and stability, a quiet reminder that we can rely on Him fully. When we're surrounded by choices or decisions that feel overwhelming, this steady voice cuts through the noise, offering clarity and wisdom that we couldn't find on our own. It doesn't add pressure or anxiety; instead, it helps us feel grounded, reminding us that we are walking with Someone who cares about us deeply and wants only the best for us. The Shepherd's voice doesn't criticize or judge us for feeling lost or unsure; rather, it meets us exactly where we are, offering gentle guidance and compassion. It's like having a close friend beside us, someone who knows us completely, who understands our fears and encourages us with patience and love. This voice is steady because it comes from a place of unwavering love and commitment. The Shepherd doesn't turn away when we struggle or stumble; instead, He speaks to us with even more gentleness, lifting us up and helping us find our way again. His voice is there in the moments of joy, celebration, and peace, but it's also there in the difficult times, the moments of pain or confusion when we might feel like giving up. No matter where we find ourselves, the Shepherd's voice is always there, inviting us to trust, to take one more step, to keep moving forward with the assurance that we are not alone. This steady voice provides the strength we need when we feel weak, the courage to face the unknown, and the hope that no matter how winding or challenging the path may be, there is purpose in every step. It encourages us to keep going, to keep growing, and to keep trusting that the Shepherd is leading us toward something good. Even when the way seems dark or the journey feels long, the Shepherd's voice is a light to our path, guiding us with a faithfulness that never changes. His voice reminds us that we are valuable, that our lives have meaning, and that we are part of a story far greater than we can see. He speaks to us in ways that reach deep into our hearts, filling us with peace and a sense of belonging. The Shepherd's voice is steady because it is grounded in a love that is unconditional and everlasting. This voice doesn't change with our circumstances or waver based on our mistakes or doubts. It is a steady presence in our lives, one that provides a foundation we can rely on, even when everything else feels uncertain. This voice invites us to rest in the knowledge that we are fully known, fully loved, and fully accepted just as we are. The Shepherd's voice calls us forward, not out of obligation or fear, but out of love and trust. It helps us to see ourselves through His eyes, to understand that we are cherished and that our journey is important to Him. As we listen to this steady voice, we find the courage to face challenges, the strength to overcome obstacles, and the peace to trust the path we are on. The Shepherd's voice is a steady reminder that we are never alone, that we are guided by a love that is greater than anything we could ever imagine. It speaks to us in the quiet moments, in the busyness of life, and in the times when we feel lost or afraid, always inviting us to trust, to listen, and to follow. His voice is the steady anchor that holds us, the light that guides us, and the love that surrounds us. It reminds us that we are part of something beautiful, something meaningful, and that every step we take is leading us closer to the heart of the Shepherd, who will never leave our side. This is the voice that says, "This is the way, walk ye in it," inviting us to journey forward with hope, peace, and the steady assurance that we are loved and guided by the Shepherd's unfailing voice.

Chapter 2 - Soothing Voice

The Shepherd's voice is a soothing voice, one that calls to us gently, saying, "Come unto me, all ye that labour and are heavy laden, and I will give you rest." Imagine the comfort in those words, spoken by someone who knows every burden you carry and every worry that weighs on your heart. Life can be filled with stress, fear, and moments when we feel like we're carrying the weight of the world on our shoulders. We try to stay strong, to keep pushing forward, but sometimes it feels like we're alone, facing struggles we weren't meant to bear on our own. That's when the Shepherd's voice breaks through, not with demands or expectations, but with a soothing, compassionate invitation to come as we are—tired, worn-out, and heavy-hearted. His voice isn't just offering a quick fix or a moment of relief; it's offering a deep, soul-restoring rest that fills every part of us with peace. The Shepherd's voice understands that we all face things that drain us, things that keep us awake at night, worried about tomorrow or struggling with pain from yesterday. This voice knows our silent battles, the ones we don't always share with others, and instead of expecting us to fight alone, it reaches out to us with open arms, welcoming us into a place of safety and care. It's like finally finding a place where we can let down our guard, where we don't have to pretend we're fine or hide how tired we feel. The Shepherd's voice soothes us by reminding us that we don't have to be perfect or strong to be worthy of rest. We don't have to prove ourselves or carry on in silence, pretending that everything is okay. Instead, we're invited to lay down the things that weigh us down, to find peace in knowing that there's Someone who is more than capable of carrying the burdens that feel too heavy for us. This invitation to rest is about so much more than just physical relaxation; it's a chance for our hearts and minds to be renewed, for the knots of worry and fear that we carry inside to slowly loosen as we breathe in the peace that the Shepherd offers. His voice tells us that it's okay to need help, to need a place where we can let go of everything that's been holding us back. We don't have to keep running on empty or pushing ourselves beyond our limits because the Shepherd sees us, understands us, and deeply cares for us. There's a tenderness in His voice, a genuine love that wants what's best for us, and He knows that the best thing for us isn't to keep carrying these burdens alone but to find rest in His presence. This soothing voice reminds us that we don't have to be defined by our struggles or weighed down by our fears. It's a voice that invites us into a relationship where we can be honest about our weaknesses, where we can admit that we're tired, and where we can find strength in knowing we're not alone. Even when the world feels overwhelming or when our problems seem too big, the Shepherd's voice is a constant reminder that there is a place of peace waiting for us, a place where we are fully known, fully loved, and fully accepted just as we are. His voice soothes us by reminding us that rest isn't something we have to earn; it's something He freely offers out of His love for us. He doesn't want us to be burned out or broken down by the pressures we face; instead, He calls us to Himself, to a place where we can find relief from the things that exhaust us. The Shepherd's voice speaks directly to our souls, filling us with a peace that goes beyond words, a calm that reaches down to the deepest parts of who we are. It's a voice that meets us in our pain, in our confusion, and in our struggles, and it speaks words of life, comfort, and hope that help us to see that we are not forgotten, not overlooked. We are precious in His sight, and He is always ready to give us the rest we need. This voice doesn't come with conditions or demands; it simply invites us to trust, to come close, and to find healing in His presence. The Shepherd knows that life can be hard and that we can feel overwhelmed by everything we face, but He doesn't leave us to manage it on our own. His voice is a refuge, a place of safety where we can be real about our needs and find comfort in the knowledge that we are deeply cared for. This soothing voice calls us to let go of our worries, to release our anxieties, and to rest in the assurance that He is with us, guiding us, and taking care of us. When we listen to this voice, we find ourselves able to breathe easier, to let go of the weight we've been carrying, and to trust that we are held in the arms of a Shepherd who will never let us down. His voice gives us permission to stop striving, to stop trying to do everything on our own, and to simply rest in His love. In a world that often demands so much from us, the Shepherd's voice stands as a steady, soothing reminder that we are loved just as we are and that we have a place where we can find true peace. This voice is more than just words; it is a promise of care, a promise that we don't have to be strong all the time, that we don't have to carry everything alone. The Shepherd's voice is always there, always ready to bring us back to a place of peace and rest, reminding us that we are never too far gone, never too broken, and never beyond His reach. His voice is a constant invitation to come close, to be renewed, and to find the rest we've been searching for, a rest that only He can give. And so, when we hear the Shepherd calling, "Come unto me," we know that we are being welcomed into a place of healing, hope, and restoration, where every burden can be laid down, and every worry can find peace. This is the gift of the Shepherd's soothing voice—a place of rest for our souls, a place of love that never ends, and a place of comfort that always waits for us, no matter where we are or what we are going through.

Chapter 3 - Summoning Voice

The Shepherd's voice is a summoning voice, one that calls to each of us with a love so deep and true that it reaches right to the core of who we are. Imagine the power of hearing a voice that knows you completely—your strengths, weaknesses, every worry, every hope, and even the secrets you keep hidden inside. This voice, the voice of Jesus, our Great Shepherd, is not just any voice; it is the voice of Someone who loves you beyond words, someone who calls you by name because you matter to Him in a way that no one else can. When He says, "My sheep hear my voice, and I know them, and they follow me," He's not speaking to strangers but to people He deeply cherishes. His voice is familiar, like the voice of a trusted friend who has always been there, even when you didn't notice. It's a voice that doesn't just want something from you but wants something for you—a life of peace, purpose, and love that you don't have to chase on your own. This summoning voice doesn't force or demand; it calls gently, with compassion and understanding, inviting you to come close, to follow, to trust, and to rest in His care. It's a voice that knows the challenges you face, the uncertainties, and the fears that sometimes fill your mind. The Shepherd doesn't call you without purpose; His voice has a reason for every step, a path that He has already walked, a journey that He has carefully planned just for you. When you hear His voice, it's like a light turning on in the darkness, showing you that you are not alone, that you have a place where you belong, and that you are valued beyond measure. He calls you because He wants you near, because His love for you is so immense that He wants to be part of every moment of your life, guiding, comforting, and providing for you. This voice isn't just a whisper in the wind; it's a promise, a pledge of His faithfulness, saying that no matter where you go or what you face, He will be there, leading you with care. His summoning voice tells you that you don't have to wander through life without direction or struggle through hardships without help. It's like a steady, loving hand reaching out, offering to walk beside you, showing you the way and keeping you safe. When He calls you, He's not just saying, "Follow me" as a command; He's inviting you into a relationship where you are fully known, fully loved, and never alone. He knows that life can be overwhelming, that the pressures and challenges of the world can sometimes make us feel small or insignificant, but His voice reminds us that we are cherished, that we have a purpose, and that we belong to Him. Even when you feel lost, or when you've made mistakes, His voice doesn't scold or push you away; it calls to you with patience and kindness, saying, "Come back to me, I am here, and I have never stopped loving you." This summoning voice is a gentle guide through every high and low, every joy and sorrow, offering comfort and strength whenever you need it. It's a voice that speaks to you not only in times of quiet but also in the midst of chaos, in the noise of everyday life, calling you to focus, to listen, and to trust that He has a plan for you. Following His voice isn't about being perfect or always knowing the right thing to do; it's about being willing to take each step in faith, believing that He will guide you, that He will help you, and that He will never leave you on your own. His voice is different from all others because it comes from a place of pure, unchanging love, a love that doesn't depend on what you can do or who you pretend to be. This voice speaks to the real you, the you that sometimes feels uncertain or afraid, and it says, "You are mine, and I will never let you go." The Shepherd's voice doesn't just speak; it heals, it restores, it reassures, and it fills you with a peace that cannot be found anywhere else. When He calls, it's a reminder that you are part of His flock, that you have a Shepherd who sees you, who knows you, and who will do anything to protect and guide you. He doesn't just want you to follow because He has authority; He wants you to follow because He loves you and knows that with Him, you are safe, cherished, and secure. This summoning voice lifts you out of fear and uncertainty, calling you to a life where you are never alone, never forgotten, and always cared for. When you hear His voice, it's like hearing the promise of a safe harbor in the middle of a storm, a place where you can find rest, courage, and hope. The Shepherd's call is a gift, a lifeline, a loving invitation to walk through life with a companion who understands you completely and wants only the best for you. It's a voice that says, "Come, follow me," not as a rule to be obeyed but as a path to be embraced, a journey where every step is watched over, every worry is shared, and every challenge is faced together.

When you follow His voice, you find yourself surrounded by a love so deep, so compassionate, that it changes everything. You realize that you don't have to carry your burdens alone, that you don't have to be strong all the time because you have a Shepherd who is strong for you. His voice is steady, gentle, and full of grace, guiding you with a wisdom that knows no end and a kindness that has no limits. The Shepherd's summoning voice doesn't just call you for today; it calls you for a lifetime, offering you a love that is eternal, a guidance that never fades, and a peace that is beyond understanding. When you hear His voice, you find a purpose that fills your heart, a belonging that settles your soul, and a hope that gives you strength for whatever lies ahead. This is the power of the Shepherd's summoning voice—a voice that knows you fully, loves you deeply, and calls you to a life that is filled with meaning, peace, and unbreakable love. So when you hear that voice, gentle yet powerful, calling you by name, know that you are being invited into something beautiful, something safe, something true, and that following this voice will lead you to a life where you are never alone, never unloved, and always held close by the Shepherd who treasures you beyond measure.

Chapter 4 - Shielding Voice

The Shepherd's voice is a shielding voice, one that surrounds us with strength and comfort, saying, "Fear thou not; for I am with thee: be not dismayed; for I am thy God." These words are like a warm, protective embrace in moments when we feel afraid or alone, offering a safe haven from life's worries and struggles. Imagine the peace that comes when you hear this voice, knowing that you are not alone in whatever you face. The Shepherd is not just beside you—He is actively guarding you, watching over every step you take with a love that will never leave you vulnerable or unprotected. Life is full of moments that challenge our courage and bring uncertainty into our hearts. Whether it's a personal struggle, a difficult decision, or a fear of the unknown, we all face things that seem bigger than we can handle. But the Shepherd's shielding voice reminds us that we don't have to handle these things alone. His voice is like a fortress, a solid rock on which we can lean, telling us to let go of our fears because He is here, holding us securely. He doesn't ask us to ignore our fears or pretend that we aren't struggling; instead, He steps into those very fears with us, assuring us that His strength is greater than anything we could ever face. When He says, "Be not dismayed; for I am thy God," it's a reminder that we are not only loved but also deeply valued by the One who has power over all things. This voice tells us that no matter how big or small our fears are, they matter to Him, and He will not let us face them alone. His shielding voice is filled with compassion and understanding, knowing exactly what we need, whether it's courage to face a challenge or peace to calm our anxieties. The Shepherd knows our hearts intimately; He knows our worries before we even say them, and His voice reaches out to us in those moments, saying, "Fear thou not." It's like having a close friend who is always by our side, someone who knows us completely and who loves us so deeply that He would do anything to protect us. This voice is steady and unwavering, offering reassurance that does not depend on our own strength but on His limitless power. We don't have to be strong all on our own; we just have to trust in the Shepherd's strength and let His voice be our shield. His voice doesn't just calm our fears; it empowers us to move forward, even when the path ahead seems difficult. With each word, He infuses us with a courage that isn't forced or shallow but deeply rooted in His promise to be with us. When He says, "I am thy God," it is a powerful reminder that we belong to Him, that we are His, and because of this, we are shielded by His love. This shielding voice doesn't mean we won't face challenges or feel fear, but it means we don't have to face them in despair or isolation. We have a God who stands with us, who fights for us, and who never leaves our side. His presence is our protection, His voice our constant reminder that no matter what life throws our way, we are never beyond His reach. Even in our weakest moments, when we feel like we can't go on, the Shepherd's voice gives us strength. It says, "Fear not," and we find the courage to take one more step, to hold on just a little longer, knowing that He is with us. His voice shields us from despair, from the lie that we are alone or unloved, and fills us with the assurance that we are seen, known, and cherished. In a world that can sometimes feel harsh and uncaring, the Shepherd's shielding voice is a soft place to land, a reminder that there is Someone who cares about every detail of our lives and who will never leave us unguarded. His voice shields us from fear by reminding us of His power, His love, and His commitment to us. He is not a distant or indifferent protector; He is deeply invested in our lives, watching over us with a love that is fierce and unbreakable. When we hear His voice, it's like a light in the darkness, guiding us and protecting us from harm. The Shepherd doesn't promise that life will always be easy, but He does promise that He will always be with us. His shielding voice gives us the confidence to face life's storms, knowing that we are never alone, never forgotten, and never without hope. So, when you feel afraid or overwhelmed, remember the Shepherd's words: "Fear thou not; for I am with thee." Let those words be the shield that guards your heart, the comfort that calms your soul, and the strength that lifts you up. The Shepherd's voice is your safe place, your constant protection, and your reminder that, no matter what, you are loved beyond measure.

Chapter 5 - Sovereign Voice

The Shepherd's voice is a sovereign voice, a voice that speaks with authority, wisdom, and love, guiding us with words that are powerful and true. When we hear, "Whatsoever he saith unto you, do it," we are reminded that this voice doesn't just offer advice or suggestions—it offers guidance that comes from the One who knows all things, sees all paths, and loves us with a love that is both gentle and strong. Imagine being able to hear the voice of someone who not only understands every detail of your life but also sees the full picture of your journey, including the things you cannot see. The Shepherd's voice is that kind of voice. It's the voice of Jesus, our Great Shepherd, who calls us to trust Him completely, to listen closely, and to follow His words with faith and courage. When He speaks to us, He isn't just giving us commands; He is giving us directions that lead to peace, to purpose, and to a life filled with His presence. His words are not burdensome or harsh; they are words spoken with love, guiding us on the right path, protecting us from harm, and leading us to places of growth and blessing. His voice is sovereign because it is above all other voices, and it calls us to listen with an open heart, to believe that He knows what is best for us, and to act on His guidance without hesitation. This isn't always easy because, sometimes, what He asks of us might feel challenging or outside our comfort zone, but His sovereign voice assures us that whatever He says is for our good. He doesn't ask us to follow Him blindly; He invites us to follow Him with trust, knowing that every word He speaks is grounded in His perfect love and His deep understanding of our hearts. When we hear Him say, "Do it," it's an invitation to step forward in faith, to take His hand, and to walk the path He has prepared for us, even if it feels uncertain or difficult. His sovereign voice is a source of strength, especially when we feel weak or unsure, reminding us that we don't have to know all the answers or see the whole picture. We only need to listen and obey, trusting that He will take care of the rest. His voice gives us courage to face our fears, to let go of our doubts, and to believe that He is with us in every step we take. The Shepherd's sovereign voice is a voice of assurance, letting us know that we are not left to figure things out on our own. He doesn't abandon us or leave us to wander in confusion; instead, He speaks to us with clarity, with conviction, and with a gentle firmness that brings peace to our hearts. He calls us to do whatever He says, not because He wants to control us but because He wants to lead us to a life that is full of joy, meaning, and love. His voice is a guiding light in a world that often feels chaotic and uncertain, showing us the way forward, helping us to make choices that align with His will and bring us closer to Him. When He says, "Do it," He is inviting us to trust His wisdom, to rely on His strength, and to believe that His plans for us are good. The Shepherd's voice doesn't just tell us what to do; it walks with us as we do it, giving us the courage, the grace, and the support we need to follow His path. He understands our weaknesses, our fears, and our struggles, and He speaks to us in a way that meets us right where we are. His sovereign voice doesn't overwhelm us; it empowers us, filling us with a sense of purpose and direction that we can't find anywhere else. In those moments when we might feel unsure or hesitant, His voice gently encourages us to take a step of faith, to believe in His promises, and to follow Him with a heart that is open and willing. His voice is a steady anchor in the storms of life, a constant reminder that we are not alone and that we are guided by a love that is strong, steadfast, and true. When He speaks, His words are like a compass, pointing us toward hope, peace, and a life that is rich with His presence. His sovereign voice calls us to surrender our fears, to trust in His goodness, and to walk forward with confidence, knowing that He will never lead us astray. When we hear, "Whatsoever he saith unto you, do it," it's more than a command—it's an invitation to enter into a deeper relationship with the Shepherd, to experience His love in a way that changes us, strengthens us, and fills us with peace. His voice is a gift, a source of wisdom and love that leads us toward a life that is full of His grace. It doesn't mean the path will always be easy, but it does mean we will never have to walk it alone. The Shepherd's sovereign voice is a promise that we are seen, known, and guided by the One who holds all things in His hands, the One who loves us more than we could ever imagine. His voice calls us to trust, to listen, and to obey, knowing that each step we take in response to His words brings us closer to Him, closer to a life of peace, and closer to the purpose He has for us. And so, when you hear His voice, saying, "Do it," let it be a reminder that you are being led by a voice of love, a voice of wisdom, and a voice that will never fail you. His sovereign voice is a gift, a treasure, and a guiding light, leading you always to a life that is full of His presence, His peace, and His unending love.

Chapter 6 - Sharpening Voice

The Shepherd's voice is a sharpening voice, one that speaks to us not just with comfort and guidance but with a loving firmness that shapes and strengthens us. When we hear the words, "As many as I love, I rebuke and chasten," it's clear that His love isn't a passive love; it's active, deeply invested, and always seeking our best. This is the voice of Jesus, our Great Shepherd, who loves us too much to leave us as we are, who sees not only who we are today but who we have the potential to become. His voice is sharpening because it helps us grow, even when that growth is challenging. Imagine a loving parent or a close friend who tells you the truth, even when it's hard to hear, not to hurt you but to help you. This is the Shepherd's way—He doesn't shy away from guiding us on a better path, even if it means correcting us along the way. His voice doesn't scold us out of frustration or anger but instead speaks with a firm gentleness, like a master craftsman refining a piece of art, removing what isn't needed to reveal the beauty and strength underneath. His rebuke isn't meant to make us feel small or worthless; rather, it's a call to rise up to the fullness of who we're meant to be. It's His way of saying, "I see so much in you, so much potential, so much goodness, and I want to help you bring it out." The Shepherd's voice is sharpening because He knows that true love sometimes requires hard truths. It's a love that isn't afraid to guide us away from things that might harm us or to correct us when we stray. Even though it can be uncomfortable to face these moments, the Shepherd's voice always corrects with love and respect. He sees the weaknesses that we might not even notice, the habits that hold us back, and the fears that limit us. And so, He speaks into these areas with a voice that is gentle yet clear, leading us away from what holds us down and toward what lifts us up. His voice reminds us that being sharpened isn't about punishment but about growth, about becoming stronger and more capable of facing life's challenges. Just as a knife needs sharpening to be effective, we need guidance and correction to live fully and wisely. When He rebukes or corrects us, it's not a sign of rejection; it's actually a sign of deep care. The Shepherd wouldn't take the time to refine us if we weren't precious to Him, if He didn't see immense value in us. His sharpening voice builds us up even as it calls us to let go of things that no longer serve us. When He challenges us, it's like He's holding up a mirror, showing us not only who we are but who we can become. His voice says, "I know it's hard, but trust Me; I'm helping you to grow, to be better, to be free from anything that keeps you from the life I have planned for you." The Shepherd's voice isn't afraid of our messiness, our mistakes, or our flaws; instead, it reaches into those very places with a love that is determined to see us through. His rebuke is like a steady hand on our shoulder, guiding us back when we wander too close to danger or when we settle for less than we deserve. His chastening isn't meant to make us feel bad about ourselves; it's meant to remind us that we are capable of more, that there's a path of wisdom, strength, and purpose waiting for us if we are willing to listen and follow. The Shepherd's voice sharpens us because He knows that life isn't always easy, that there are trials and tests that require resilience and wisdom. By refining us, He's preparing us, equipping us with the strength we'll need to face the challenges ahead. This sharpening voice isn't harsh or critical; it's encouraging, urging us to rise to the challenges of life with courage and integrity. Every time He corrects us, it's as though He's saying, "I believe in you, and I'm here to help you grow." This voice helps us to see the areas in our lives that need growth, not so we can feel discouraged, but so we can make real changes that lead to a life of greater peace, purpose, and fulfillment. The Shepherd's voice calls us to leave behind old habits, fears, and doubts, helping us to become more of who we were created to be. His rebuke may sting at times, but it's always followed by grace and encouragement, showing us that we are never alone in this process. He walks with us, guiding us, supporting us, and giving us the strength to keep moving forward. His sharpening voice reminds us that we are loved deeply, loved enough for Him to want the best for us, even if it means calling us to hard truths and necessary changes. It's a love that cares too much to stay silent when we're heading down a harmful path or settling for less than the life He has for us. In those moments of rebuke, He doesn't leave us feeling judged or condemned; instead, He fills us with hope and a vision for a brighter future. This voice is always lifting us up, helping us to see that the path of growth, though challenging, is also deeply rewarding. The Shepherd's sharpening voice is one of the greatest gifts we could receive because it leads us to a life of strength, integrity, and joy. It teaches us to embrace change, to welcome growth, and to trust that even in the refining moments, we are being guided by a hand that holds us with love. So, when you hear the Shepherd's voice speaking words that might challenge or correct you, remember that these words come from a place of love and a desire to see you become all that you can be. This is the voice that calls us to be brave, to let go of what no longer serves us, and to step into a future shaped by His love, wisdom, and unwavering commitment to our growth. His sharpening voice is a voice of hope, a promise that we are not only loved as we are but also loved enough to be guided toward something greater. It's a voice that says, "I am with you, every step of the way, helping you to grow, to learn, and to become all that I have created you to be."

Chapter 7 - Strengthening Voice

The Shepherd's voice is a strengthening voice, one that speaks to us with love, courage, and an unshakable promise that brings comfort to our souls. When we hear Him say, "Be of good cheer; I have overcome the world," it's more than just words—it's a reassurance from Someone who understands every challenge, every fear, and every worry we face. Imagine facing something that feels overwhelming, something that weighs on your heart and makes you feel small or powerless. In those moments, the Shepherd's voice speaks clearly and powerfully, reminding us that no matter how tough life gets, He has already overcome it all. His words tell us that we are not alone in our struggles, that we don't have to carry our burdens by ourselves. He has gone before us, facing all the trials and hardships of life, and He emerged victorious. This voice isn't one that merely sympathizes with us from a distance—it is a voice that knows intimately what it feels like to face hardship, pain, and suffering. Jesus, our Great Shepherd, doesn't speak from a place of distant authority but from a place of deep understanding and compassion. He knows the weight of what we carry because He has carried it too, and when He says, "Be of good cheer," it's an invitation to find strength in His victory, to remember that His love has already conquered everything we might face. The Shepherd's voice strengthens us by filling us with courage, a courage that isn't forced or fake, but a real confidence that grows from trusting in Someone greater than ourselves. We don't have to be strong on our own because He is our strength, and He offers it freely, without judgment or hesitation. When we feel weak, uncertain, or afraid, His voice comes like a gentle but firm reminder that we are held by a love that will not let us fall. It's as if He's saying, "I know it's hard, but you are not alone—I am with you, and I will see you through." His words remind us that the struggles we face do not define us and that our worth isn't tied to our ability to be strong all the time. Instead, He calls us to lean on Him, to find strength in

His presence, and to trust that He has already overcome every obstacle. The Shepherd's voice doesn't deny the reality of our pain or the hardships we face, but it lifts our hearts, helping us to see beyond the immediate struggles to the promise of victory and peace. He doesn't ask us to ignore our fears but instead to bring them to Him, to allow His voice to fill the places in our hearts that feel empty or weary. This voice strengthens us by reminding us of the bigger picture, that we are part of a story that ends in victory, peace, and joy because of Him. When He says, "I have overcome the world," it's not just a statement—it's a promise that gives us hope, a reason to keep going even when the road feels long. The Shepherd's voice helps us to stand tall, to face each day with a renewed sense of purpose, knowing that His love surrounds us, His strength upholds us, and His promises will never fail. This strengthening voice isn't just there in the easy moments; it's there especially when life feels hardest, when we feel weakest, and when we're not sure how to take the next step. In those times, His voice is a rock, a steady foundation we can lean on, giving us the confidence to keep moving forward. He tells us that we don't have to have it all figured out, that we don't have to be perfect, because His love is enough, His strength is enough, and His victory is enough. This is the voice of a Shepherd who knows us completely and loves us fully, who wants to see us grow, thrive, and experience the fullness of life even in the midst of trials. When we listen to His voice, we find a peace that doesn't make sense by the world's standards, a peace that holds us steady in the middle of storms. His words don't just inspire us; they fill us with a real, lasting strength that can face any challenge, any heartbreak, and any fear. The Shepherd's voice is a constant source of encouragement, reminding us that we are never alone, that we are never without hope, and that we are always deeply loved. His strengthening voice helps us to see ourselves through His eyes, to understand that we are capable, that we are worthy, and that we have a purpose because of His love. Every time He speaks, it's like a reminder that we are not defined by our failures, our fears, or our limitations but by His victory, His peace, and His grace. This voice doesn't ask us to be strong all the time; it simply invites us to rest in the strength of the Shepherd, to trust that He will carry us when we can't carry ourselves. When He says, "Be of good cheer," it's a call to lift our heads, to see beyond the present struggles, and to trust that brighter days are ahead because of His promises. The Shepherd's voice strengthens us by giving us hope, by filling us with a courage that is gentle but unwavering, and by reminding us that we are part of something greater than ourselves. In His presence, we find a strength that isn't about denying our pain but about rising above it, about finding peace in knowing that no matter what happens, He is with us. His voice calls us to live with confidence, to move forward with courage, and to trust that His love will see us through. This is the power of the Shepherd's voice—it doesn't just comfort; it empowers, it lifts us up, and it helps us to become who we were created to be. So when you hear His voice, saying, "Be of good cheer; I have overcome the world," let it be a reminder that you are loved, that you are strong because He is strong, and that you are never alone. His voice is a gift, a source of unending strength and hope, a constant reminder that no matter what we face, we are held in the loving hands of a Shepherd who has already won the victory for us.

Chapter 8 - Showing Voice

The Shepherd's voice is a showing voice, a voice that gently guides, teaches, and leads us through life's twists and turns with patience and clarity. When we pray, "Teach me thy way, O Lord, and lead me in a plain path," we're asking for a kind of guidance that goes beyond simple directions; we're asking for wisdom, understanding, and a deep sense of trust in the Shepherd's ability to show us the way we should go. Imagine the comfort of knowing that no matter how confusing or challenging life becomes, there is a voice that can lead us, a voice that knows every step of the journey and wants only the best for us. This voice doesn't push or rush us; instead, it walks with us, meeting us at each point in life and showing us the path forward, even when we can't see very far ahead. It's like walking through a foggy forest but feeling the gentle, guiding hand of the Shepherd on your shoulder, reassuring you that you're not alone and that He knows the way. The Shepherd's voice is patient and understanding, knowing that we may not always see the path clearly or feel confident in our choices. When He speaks, He doesn't simply give commands or issue orders; He teaches us, helping us to understand not only where we are going but why each step matters. His voice shows us the way, not just with words but with love and wisdom, shaping our hearts to be open to His guidance. The path He leads us on is often a journey of growth, where we learn not just the destination but the character, faith, and trust we need to reach it. His showing voice gently corrects us when we go astray, not with harshness but with a steady and caring call to return to the right path. It's as if He's saying, "This is the way, walk ye in it," and each time we listen, we find that our steps become a little lighter, our hearts a little braver, and our faith a little stronger. His voice doesn't ignore our fears or doubts but patiently helps us to move beyond them, teaching us that we don't have to understand everything right away or have all the answers ourselves. We are invited to trust that He sees what we cannot and that His wisdom is greater than any fear or confusion we might feel. The Shepherd's showing voice is a voice of peace, a voice that calls us to walk on a plain path, a path that, even if it feels difficult, is filled with His presence, His love, and His assurance that we are never alone. When we ask Him to lead us, we're opening ourselves to the kind of guidance that is rooted in His love, a love that wants nothing but good for us, even if the journey requires patience, faith, and courage. His voice is like a light in the darkness, showing us where to place each step, not with the demand to be perfect but with the invitation to trust and follow. He knows the places where we feel uncertain, the moments when we feel lost, and the fears that sometimes cloud our vision. And in each of those moments, His voice is there, showing us a little more of the path, encouraging us to take one more step, and reminding us that He will never let us walk alone. His showing voice is a gentle reminder that we don't have to be perfect travelers; we only need to be willing to listen and to learn. The Shepherd teaches us not just through words but through His presence, His patience, and His constant willingness to walk with us, no matter how winding the path may be. He doesn't grow weary of our questions or frustrated with our need for reassurance; instead, He embraces every step of our journey, guiding us with a love that is patient and kind. His showing voice calls us to see ourselves as He sees us—capable of growth, worthy of love, and deserving of the guidance that only He can provide. As we follow His voice, we learn that the plain path isn't always the easiest path, but it is the one filled with His presence, His peace, and His promise to be with us every step of the way. His voice doesn't just show us the way; it helps us become stronger, wiser, and more compassionate along the journey. We begin to see that each step, each lesson, each moment of trust, is shaping us into the people we were created to be. The Shepherd's showing voice is a gift, a blessing, and a promise that we are never left to wander alone. So, when you hear His voice, saying, "Teach me thy way," know that it's an invitation to walk closely with Him, to learn from His wisdom, and to trust that the path He shows is one of love, purpose, and unending grace. His showing voice is there to guide, to comfort, and to lead us to a life that is not only safe but filled with His presence, His peace, and His everlasting love.

Chapter 9 - Soothing Voice of Healing

The Shepherd's voice is a soothing voice of healing, a voice that reaches into the deepest places of our hearts with comfort, peace, and the power to make us whole again. When we hear the words, "I am the Lord that healeth thee," it's like a gentle touch that tells us that no matter what wounds we carry—whether they are wounds of the body, the mind, or the spirit—there is Someone who cares deeply about our pain and is here to bring us healing. Imagine carrying a hurt that feels too heavy, something that weighs on your heart and makes you feel like you're broken beyond repair. In those moments, the Shepherd's voice speaks softly, assuring us that He understands every part of what we're going through. His voice is like a balm for our soul, offering us the relief we've been longing for, telling us that we don't have to bear our pain alone. This voice doesn't rush us to feel better or pressure us to pretend that everything is okay. Instead, it meets us right where we are, in whatever state we find ourselves—tired, hurting, scared, or weak—and it whispers that healing is possible, that hope is alive, and that we are not alone. The Shepherd's voice of healing is filled with compassion because He knows our pain intimately. He understands our struggles and the weight of our burdens because He, too, has known suffering. His voice doesn't look away from our wounds or minimize our struggles; it embraces them, acknowledging the hurt while offering the promise of restoration. The healing He offers isn't just a quick fix or a surface solution; it's a deep, complete kind of healing that reaches into every part of us. This voice soothes the hurt we carry in silence, the unspoken fears and anxieties that no one else sees, and it speaks with a power that assures us that even the deepest wounds can be healed. His voice brings peace to the chaos inside us, calming the storms in our hearts and helping us breathe easier. It's a voice that says, "You are loved, just as you are, wounds and all," and that love itself begins to heal us. Sometimes the journey to healing feels long, and we may wonder if the hurt will ever truly go away. But the Shepherd's voice is patient, walking with us through every step, never rushing us but always gently encouraging us to keep moving forward, to keep hoping, to keep trusting. He doesn't promise that the healing journey will be easy, but He promises that we will not walk it alone. His voice is a steady presence, a reminder that healing is a process and that every small step we take toward wholeness matters. His voice of healing doesn't just bring relief to our wounds; it strengthens us, helping us to find meaning, resilience, and even joy along the way. The Shepherd knows that some wounds are invisible, hidden deep within our hearts, and that these are often the hardest to heal. His voice reaches into those hidden places, offering comfort where we thought no comfort could reach, and hope where we thought hope was lost. He sees the broken pieces we try to hide, the parts of ourselves we think are unworthy of love, and His voice assures us that there is nothing too broken for Him to mend. The healing He offers is one of wholeness, not just physical relief but a deep renewal that restores our sense of peace, purpose, and self-worth. His voice doesn't judge us for our pain or blame us for our wounds; instead, it lifts us up, offering a safe place where we can be vulnerable, where we can lay down our burdens and let His love cover our hurt. The Shepherd's voice tells us that healing is not about forgetting our pain but about finding peace within it, about discovering that even our wounds have a place in His story of love and redemption. His voice is gentle but strong, full of a compassion that does not fade or falter. He is a healer who does not get tired of our need or frustrated with our struggles. His voice encourages us to trust in the healing process, to believe that every step, however small, brings us closer to wholeness. This is a healing that respects our journey, that gives us room to breathe and time to heal without pressure. When He says, "I am the Lord that healeth thee," it's more than a promise—it's an embrace that wraps around us, reminding us that we are cared for, valued, and cherished, even in our brokenness. His voice teaches us that healing is possible, that pain does not define us, and that we are never beyond the reach of His love. The Shepherd's voice of healing invites us to let go of the guilt or shame we might feel about our wounds, to stop feeling like we have to carry the weight alone. He knows that some pains are not easily seen by others, and He speaks directly to those hidden parts of us, offering compassion that brings tears of relief because we finally feel understood. His voice doesn't just tell us to feel better; it patiently walks with us through the hard work of healing, through the times when it feels like progress is slow or setbacks are painful. And when we falter, His voice is there, lifting us up, reminding us that it's okay to rest, that healing is not a race but a journey that He will walk with us every step of the way. The Shepherd's voice is like a light that breaks through the darkness of our hurt, a gentle assurance that the worst parts of our story do not have to be the end. His voice of healing calls us toward a future where our wounds are no longer chains that hold us back but are transformed into marks of strength and growth. He doesn't erase our past or pretend the pain never happened; instead, He brings meaning to it, showing us that even in our hurt, we are deeply loved, seen, and valued. This voice of healing calls us to be patient with ourselves, to trust in the process, and to believe that with time, love, and grace, we will heal. It tells us that our wounds do not make us less worthy; they simply make us more in need of His love, a love that is always available, always reaching out, and always ready to bring peace. His voice is there in our darkest nights, in the quiet moments when the pain feels too much to bear, and it speaks softly, "I am with you, I am healing you." His voice is a constant reminder that healing is not only possible but promised, that we are cared for by a Shepherd who will never leave our side, who will hold us through every moment of hurt, and who will bring us through to a place of peace, joy, and wholeness once again. His voice of healing is a beautiful gift, a powerful reminder that no wound is too deep for His love, and that no hurt is beyond His power to heal. So when we hear Him say, "I am the Lord that healeth thee," let it sink into our hearts as a soothing balm, a reminder that we are loved, cherished, and safe in the care of a Shepherd who will never give up on bringing us to a place of complete and lasting healing.

Chapter 10 - Soul-Restoring Voice

The Shepherd's voice is a soul-restoring voice, one that reaches into the tired, weary places of our hearts and breathes life back into us. When we hear, "He restoreth my soul: he leadeth me in the paths of righteousness," it's like a gentle, refreshing breeze that sweeps away all the heaviness, worry, and weariness that we've been carrying. Imagine feeling weighed down by life—burdened by responsibilities, disappointments, and perhaps even a sadness that no one else sees—and then hearing a voice that says, "I am here to restore you." This voice, the voice of Jesus, is like a healing balm for our souls, bringing back peace, joy, and a sense of purpose when we feel drained. It doesn't just lift us up for a moment; it fills us with a lasting strength that renews us from the inside out. The Shepherd's voice doesn't overlook our pain or minimize our struggles; instead, it acknowledges them, understands them, and offers true restoration that goes beyond a quick fix. His voice reaches into the parts of us that are broken or tired and whispers words of comfort and encouragement, reminding us that we are not alone. When life feels like a constant uphill climb, His soul-restoring voice invites us to rest in His presence, to let go of our burdens, and to trust that He is here to guide us back to a place of peace. He doesn't just put a bandage on our wounds; He heals us, bringing us back to a place of wholeness and joy. His voice is like a river that gently flows into the dry places of our hearts, refreshing and reviving us in ways we didn't even know we needed. The Shepherd's voice restores us by reminding us of who we truly are—His beloved, His cherished, His chosen ones—and He leads us on paths that bring us closer to Him and to the life we were meant to live. Sometimes, we lose sight of ourselves, feeling defined by our mistakes, our fears, or the pressures around us, but His soul-restoring voice calls us back to our true identity, an identity that is rooted in His love. This voice is like a light in the darkness, gently guiding us back to a place of peace, purpose, and righteousness.

When He leads us on paths of righteousness, it's not about demanding perfection or setting impossible standards; it's about guiding us to a life that brings us true fulfillment and joy. His voice leads us away from paths that drain us or harm us and guides us toward choices that bring life, growth, and hope. This is not the voice of harsh demands or criticism; it is the voice of a Shepherd who deeply cares for His flock and wants each one to find rest, joy, and purpose. His soul-restoring voice meets us exactly where we are, whether we're struggling, lost, or feeling far from who we're meant to be. He doesn't push us to move faster than we're ready for; instead, He walks with us, step by step, restoring our strength and guiding us gently toward wholeness. The Shepherd's voice knows that life can sometimes feel overwhelming and that our souls can grow weary from the demands and hardships we face. His voice calls us to come and find rest, to let go of the things that weigh us down, and to allow Him to renew our spirit. He doesn't ignore the pain we feel or the struggles we face; He acknowledges them and offers us a safe place where we can be vulnerable, honest, and open. His voice reassures us that it's okay to need rest, that it's okay to feel tired, and that there is no shame in seeking renewal from the One who loves us most. When He says, "I restore your soul," He is offering us a gift, a beautiful promise that we don't have to do it all on our own. The Shepherd's voice is a constant presence, a source of comfort and strength that we can lean on whenever we feel weary or lost. He knows every corner of our hearts, every fear, every worry, and every hope, and He speaks to each one with a tenderness that reminds us of our worth. His soul-restoring voice doesn't just make us feel better temporarily; it brings a lasting peace that stays with us, filling us with a strength and courage we didn't know we had. In His care, we are not just surviving; we are thriving, finding new life, new hope, and new joy every day. The Shepherd's voice doesn't just restore our souls; it renews our sense of purpose, reminding us that we are part of something greater, something beautiful, something eternal. He calls us to follow paths that bring life, paths that lead us closer to Him, and paths that fill us with joy and peace. This voice doesn't lead us astray; it guides us in the way of righteousness, the way of love, compassion, and kindness. His voice calls us to be the best version of ourselves, not because we have to earn His love but because we are already deeply loved. When He speaks, His words are like a gentle hand on our shoulder, a comforting presence that tells us we are safe, we are valued, and we are restored. The Shepherd's soul-restoring voice is a reminder that we are not defined by our past or by our struggles; we are defined by His love and His grace. No matter how far we've strayed or how lost we may feel, His voice is always calling us back, inviting us to find rest and renewal in His presence. This voice tells us that it's okay to lay down our burdens, to stop striving, and to simply be, knowing that we are cherished beyond measure. His voice is a lifeline, a source of hope that fills us with the courage to keep going, even when the road is tough. He is the Shepherd who knows every path, every twist, and every turn, and He promises to lead us in ways that bring life, joy, and peace. When we listen to His voice, we find a peace that is deeper than anything this world can offer, a peace that fills our hearts and renews our souls. The Shepherd's voice is not just a comforting presence; it's a transformative force that restores us, heals us, and makes us whole. In His voice, we find a love that is unchanging, a strength that never fades, and a hope that is eternal. His soul-restoring voice is always there, always ready to guide us, to lift us up, and to remind us that we are never alone. So, when you hear His voice saying, "I restore your soul," know that this is a promise you can hold onto, a promise that no matter where life takes you, you are loved, you are valued, and you are being led by the One who knows you best and loves you most. His voice is the anchor for our souls, the light for our path, and the comfort we need every day.

Chapter 11 - Soft Voice of Compassion

The Shepherd's voice is a soft voice of compassion, a voice so gentle and tender that it can reach the places in our hearts that are most fragile, places we may have hidden away out of fear of being hurt even more. When we hear the words, "A bruised reed shall he not break," we are reminded that the Shepherd's compassion is unlike anything we experience in the world; it is a love so kind, so understanding, that it doesn't push, pressure, or rush us when we are feeling broken, bruised, or overwhelmed. Imagine a tiny, delicate reed that has been bruised by the wind, bent, and fragile, barely holding on. Most would think it's worthless, too damaged to stand, yet the Shepherd doesn't dismiss it. He sees the bruised reed and chooses to handle it with the utmost care, carefully holding it, gently supporting it, and giving it a chance to heal and grow strong once more. This is how He treats us when we're feeling wounded or worn out by life. The world may sometimes feel harsh, as though it only values strength and perfection, but the Shepherd values every part of us, including the parts that feel weak or damaged. His voice doesn't come with judgment or disappointment; it comes with understanding and a deep desire to comfort and restore. When we're feeling down, broken, or defeated, His soft voice of compassion reaches out to us, wrapping us in a sense of warmth and safety that lets us know we're not alone, and we're certainly not too broken for His love. His voice doesn't demand that we pick ourselves up or "get over" our struggles; instead, it meets us right where we are, acknowledging our pain and gently encouraging us to rest in His care. There is no rush in His love, no pressure to be anything more than we are in that moment. He simply wants us to know that we are seen, valued, and deeply loved, just as we are. His compassion flows to us like a gentle stream, calming the anxieties that churn within us, reminding us that it's okay to feel hurt, it's okay to be vulnerable, and it's okay to lean on Him for strength. The Shepherd's voice is like a balm to our souls, a soft whisper that says, "You are precious to Me, even in your weakness, even in your brokenness." His voice doesn't overlook our pain or try to brush it away; rather, it draws near to us, inviting us to share our burdens and to let Him carry what we can't handle on our own. In a world that often overlooks those who are hurting or expects us to always be strong, His voice stands out as a beacon of true compassion, a reminder that we don't have to pretend or hide our bruises with Him. He cares deeply about every tear, every worry, every fear, and His voice tells us that we are safe in His presence. The Shepherd's compassion is gentle and patient, understanding that healing takes time, that some wounds go deep, and that we need a space to feel loved without judgment. His voice is a constant presence, a gentle reminder that we are not burdens to Him, that we are not "too much" for Him to handle. He invites us to come as we are, with all our bruises and brokenness, and to let His love be the healing force in our lives. The Shepherd doesn't grow tired of our neediness or frustrated by our struggles; instead, He embraces every part of us with a tenderness that says, "You are worth every moment, every word, every ounce of love I have to give." His soft voice of compassion is like a shelter in a storm, a place where we can rest, let our guard down, and simply be ourselves, knowing that we are accepted and loved completely. He doesn't need us to be perfect, to be strong, or to be anything other than who we are. His love is enough to hold us in all our imperfections, and His compassion is big enough to carry us through even the darkest days. The Shepherd sees the bruises that no one else sees, the hidden hurts that we carry in silence, and He speaks to those places with a kindness that lets us know we are not forgotten or overlooked. His voice assures us that our pain matters to Him, that our struggles are important to Him, and that He will never leave us to face them alone. This soft voice of compassion doesn't force us to be anything we're not ready to be; it simply invites us to rest, to heal, and to trust that we are held in the arms of Someone who loves us beyond measure. His voice tells us that healing is a journey, and that every step, no matter how small, is a step worth taking. We don't have to be strong every moment, and we don't have to hide our wounds. The Shepherd's compassion meets us right where we are, bringing a sense of peace, comfort, and understanding that is beyond words. His voice is a safe haven, a gentle reminder that we are loved, that we are valued, and that we are never alone. When we feel like we can't go on, His voice whispers to us, giving us hope, strength, and the assurance that we are deeply cherished. His compassion is a constant, unwavering love that doesn't diminish with our weaknesses but rather draws nearer to us in our need. So when we hear His soft voice of compassion, saying, "A bruised reed shall he not break," let it remind us that we are seen, we are loved, and we are cared for by a Shepherd whose love is as gentle as it is strong. His voice is a balm for our wounds, a comfort for our hearts, and a promise that no matter how bruised we may feel, we are never beyond the reach of His compassionate love.

Chapter 12 - Sobering Voice of Warning

The Shepherd's voice is a sobering voice of warning, one that reaches out to us not with anger or harshness, but with a deep, caring concern that calls us to pay attention, to "take heed, and beware of covetousness." This voice isn't trying to frighten or judge us; it's trying to protect us from things that can slowly harm us, even if we don't realize it at first. Imagine a parent guiding a child away from a hot stove, gently but firmly warning them about the dangers they cannot yet fully understand. This is how the Shepherd speaks to us, warning us about covetousness, the desire to have more, to seek what others have, to chase after things that may look shiny or promising but often leave us empty and unsatisfied. His warning is compassionate, rooted in a love that sees the traps we sometimes set for ourselves when we allow our hearts to be consumed by wanting more—whether it's more possessions, more status, or more of anything that seems to promise happiness but ultimately cannot satisfy our souls. The Shepherd knows that covetousness is a quiet thief, one that can creep into our lives and steal our joy, our peace, and our contentment without us even realizing it. His voice, therefore, is like a light shining into our hearts, helping us see the places where we may be yearning for things that cannot truly fulfill us. It's a voice that calls us to be aware, to reflect, and to guard our hearts against the distractions and desires that may pull us away from what really matters. This sobering voice isn't here to make us feel guilty for wanting good things; rather, it gently reminds us that true happiness doesn't come from chasing after the next new thing but from finding peace and gratitude in the blessings we already have. His voice warns us because He wants us to live lives of freedom and joy, unburdened by the endless cycle of always wanting more. The Shepherd understands how easy it is for our hearts to get caught up in comparison, to look at what others have and feel that we are somehow lacking. He knows that this can lead us down a path where we lose sight of the beauty in our own lives, where we start to believe that we need more to be happy, loved, or fulfilled. His voice of warning is a call back to simplicity, to a life where we appreciate the gifts we already possess, where we find joy not in the accumulation of things but in the relationships, the experiences, and the purpose He has given us. This warning is not about denying us happiness or good things; it's about protecting our hearts from the emptiness that often follows when we place our hopes in things that are temporary or material. The Shepherd's voice calls us to "take heed" because He knows that covetousness can lead to dissatisfaction, jealousy, and even resentment. He doesn't want us to waste our lives chasing after things that, in the end, do not bring us closer to Him or to the life of peace and purpose He desires for us. Instead, His voice invites us to let go of the endless desire for more, to rest in the knowledge that we are enough, that we are loved, and that we already have all we need in Him. The warning to beware of covetousness is a gentle reminder that our true worth and happiness are not found in possessions, status, or comparisons, but in the contentment and joy that come from a heart that is grateful, humble, and free. His voice helps us to see that covetousness can be a trap, one that binds us to a life of constant striving, always looking outward instead of inward, always feeling like we are missing something when, in truth, we are already blessed. The Shepherd's warning is an invitation to a life where we don't measure our worth by what we own or achieve but by the love and peace we find in Him. He speaks to us with care, helping us to recognize the subtle ways that covetousness can sneak into our lives, clouding our vision and making us forget the value of what we already have. His voice reminds us that the joy we seek cannot be bought or earned; it is a gift that grows in a heart that is content and free from the need to constantly compare or compete. The Shepherd's warning isn't about limiting us; it's about freeing us, opening our eyes to a life where we are truly satisfied, where we are grateful for the simple things, and where we find meaning beyond material wealth or possessions. His voice is a call to guard our hearts, to recognize that the desires of this world are often fleeting, and to remember that real happiness lies in love, kindness, and faithfulness. He warns us because He wants us to live deeply, to be present with the blessings before us, and to find a joy that is not dependent on what we have but on who we are and whose we are. His voice guides us back to a path of peace, away from the stress and anxiety that often come with wanting more, reminding us that life is about connection, purpose, and love. The Shepherd's voice is a voice of wisdom, one that sees through the illusions of this world and calls us to something more meaningful. He knows that covetousness can lead us down a road where we lose sight of ourselves, where we become consumed by what we lack rather than thankful for what we have. His warning is a loving nudge to turn our focus back to what truly matters, to live in a way that is rich in spirit, not just in possessions. When He says, "Take heed, and beware of covetousness," it is a gentle yet powerful reminder that we are already loved, already enough, and that the deepest joy comes from a life that is centered in gratitude, simplicity, and love. His voice calls us to live fully, not in the pursuit of more but in the embrace of what is already ours—peace, love, and the assurance that we are deeply cherished. The Shepherd's voice of warning is a gift, a message of love that guides us toward a life of contentment, fulfillment, and true joy. In a world that constantly tells us we need more, His voice is a refreshing reminder that we have all we need in Him. His voice frees us from the chains of comparison, from the constant pressure to achieve and acquire, and leads us to a place where we can rest, be thankful, and find joy in the simple, beautiful moments of life.

Chapter 13 - Serene Voice of Peace

The Shepherd's voice is a serene voice of peace, a voice that speaks softly and gently, reaching into the depths of our hearts with a calm that nothing in this world can give. When Jesus says, "Peace I leave with you, my peace I give unto you," it's more than just words; it's a promise from the One who knows us completely, who sees our worries, our fears, and our struggles, and wants to give us a peace that fills us from the inside out. Imagine a peace that wraps around you like a warm blanket on a cold night, a peace that steadies you when everything else feels uncertain, and a peace that reassures you that no matter what happens, you are held in love. This is the peace the Shepherd offers—a kind of peace that doesn't depend on life being perfect or easy, but rather on His unwavering presence with us through it all. Life can feel chaotic and overwhelming, with so many things pulling at us, making us feel restless or anxious, but the Shepherd's voice cuts through all of that noise, inviting us to breathe, to let go of our worries, and to rest in His calm assurance. His voice is like a gentle whisper in a storm, a reminder that we don't have to have everything figured out, that we don't have to carry all of our burdens alone. This peace is not something we have to earn or strive for; it's a gift, freely given from a heart of boundless love, a love that desires only our well-being, our rest, and our joy. The Shepherd's voice brings peace because it speaks to us in our language, meeting us in our fears and gently guiding us to a place of trust, a place where we know that everything will be okay because He is with us. His peace is a steadying presence, one that grounds us, reminding us that we are not alone and that we are cared for beyond measure. When we feel uncertain about the future or weighed down by the pressures of the present, His voice calls us to lay down our worries, to surrender our fears, and to let His peace fill the empty, aching spaces within us. This voice of peace doesn't ignore our troubles or dismiss our pain; instead, it acknowledges all of it and offers us comfort, as if to say, "I am here, and I will help you through." The Shepherd knows that life brings storms, moments that test our strength and shake our hearts, but His serene voice of peace tells us that we don't have to weather those storms alone. He walks beside us, His voice a constant reminder that we are safe, that we are loved, and that we have a place to turn when life feels too heavy. His peace is like a river that flows through us, washing away the tension, the fear, and the doubts, leaving us with a sense of calm that is hard to explain yet easy to feel. This is the peace that doesn't depend on the absence of trouble but on the presence of Someone who loves us deeply and eternally. His voice calls us to stop striving, to stop trying to control every detail, and to simply rest in the knowledge that He has everything in His hands. The Shepherd's peace fills us with a quiet strength, a courage that doesn't come from being strong all the time but from knowing that we are held by the One who is stronger than anything we will ever face. When He says, "My peace I give unto you," it's an invitation to leave behind the anxieties that steal our joy, the fears that rob our rest, and the worries that cloud our hearts, and to let His peace take their place. His voice of peace is like a gentle reminder that we don't have to carry everything alone, that we have Someone who sees us, who understands us, and who will never leave our side. In a world that often feels busy, loud, and uncertain, the Shepherd's voice is a safe place, a quiet refuge where we can pause, breathe, and find the peace we so desperately need. This peace doesn't mean that all our problems will disappear, but it means that we can face them with a heart that is calm, a mind that is clear, and a spirit that is anchored in His love. His peace reminds us that we are not defined by our struggles, our fears, or our failures; we are defined by His love, a love that is constant, unchanging, and always present. The Shepherd's voice speaks peace over our lives, covering us with a grace that allows us to let go of perfection, to release the need to have everything under control, and to simply rest in His care. His voice tells us that we are enough, that we are safe, and that we are deeply loved, just as we are. This peace isn't something we can find on our own; it comes from the Shepherd who knows exactly what we need, who sees the burdens we carry, and who is always ready to take them from us. His peace is a gentle reminder that we are not alone in this journey, that we have a Companion who walks with us, holding us steady when we feel unsteady, and offering us a calm that nothing else can give. The Shepherd's peace invites us to slow down, to listen, and to trust that we are exactly where we need to be, that we are cared for, and that we have nothing to fear. When we accept His peace, we find ourselves able to face life's challenges with a quiet confidence, a trust that even in the hardest moments, we are held by a love that will never let us go. His voice of peace doesn't change our circumstances, but it changes us, giving us the strength to face whatever comes our way with a heart that is calm and a spirit that is filled with hope. The Shepherd's peace is a gentle but powerful force, one that reminds us that we are cherished, that we are valued, and that we are safe in His hands. This peace allows us to be present, to appreciate the simple, beautiful moments of life, and to find joy even in the midst of difficulties. His voice calls us to let go of our worries, to surrender our fears, and to embrace a peace that is as steady as it is gentle. This is the peace that allows us to live fully, to love deeply, and to trust completely, knowing that we are cared for by the Shepherd who loves us with an everlasting love. So when we hear His serene voice of peace, let it remind us that we are safe, that we are loved, and that we have a place to rest, no matter what life brings. His peace is a gift, a promise, and a constant presence that fills us with the quiet assurance that we are never alone and that we are always deeply cherished.

Chapter 14 - Steadfast Voice of Faithfulness

The Shepherd's voice is a steadfast voice of faithfulness, a voice that speaks with a promise that is unbreakable, saying, "I will never leave thee, nor forsake thee." This voice is like an anchor in the storm, a firm hand holding us steady when everything else feels uncertain or shaky. Imagine the strength and comfort of hearing those words, "I will never leave you," from Someone who truly understands every part of you—your strengths, your weaknesses, your worries, and your dreams. The Shepherd's voice isn't like the voices of this world that may come and go, or make promises only to break them. His voice is constant, unwavering, and full of a love that will never fade. This faithfulness is not just a feeling or a fleeting emotion; it's a promise that He keeps in every single moment, in every situation, and through every trial we face. His voice tells us that no matter how dark or difficult life may get, we are not alone. We are never left to face things by ourselves because the Shepherd is right there with us, holding our hand, guiding our steps, and giving us the strength to keep going. His faithfulness is like a warm, steady light in the darkest of nights, reassuring us that we are seen, known, and loved, even when we feel invisible or forgotten. He doesn't walk away when things get hard, and He doesn't turn His back on us when we make mistakes. His love is a love that endures all things, and His voice of faithfulness is always calling us back, gently reminding us that we are His, and nothing will ever change that. The Shepherd's voice of faithfulness means that we can count on Him, that we can trust in His promises even when life feels uncertain or people let us down. When He says, "I will never forsake you," it's a declaration that He will stand by us through thick and thin, through joy and sorrow, through success and failure. This is not a voice that demands we be perfect or never stumble; it's a voice that understands our humanity, that accepts our flaws, and loves us unconditionally. His faithfulness is a safe place where we can bring all of our fears, all of our doubts, and all of our questions, knowing that we will not be turned away. His voice is like a steady presence, a foundation that holds us up even when everything else seems to be crumbling. When we feel lost, His voice is there to guide us back, to reassure us that we are still on the path, that we are not forgotten, and that we are loved beyond measure. In times of loneliness, when we feel isolated or afraid, the Shepherd's voice whispers to us, "I am here, and I am not going anywhere." This promise of faithfulness fills us with hope, giving us the courage to face each day with the confidence that we are not walking alone. His voice is a constant reminder that we are deeply loved, not for what we can do or achieve but simply because we are His. His steadfast voice doesn't waver based on our actions or circumstances; it remains the same, a faithful presence that holds us close, no matter what. The Shepherd's faithfulness means that we don't have to be strong all the time; we can lean on Him, trusting that He will carry us when we feel weak, guide us when we feel lost, and hold us when we feel afraid. His voice is a source of strength that doesn't run out, a well of comfort that never dries up, and a promise of presence that we can rely on every single day. In a world that often feels unstable and unpredictable, His steadfast voice of faithfulness is a blessing, a gift that brings peace and assurance to our hearts. It reminds us that we are not alone, that we are seen, and that we are held in the hands of a Shepherd who will never let us go. His faithfulness is a constant presence, a love that remains even when everything else fades away. So when we hear His voice say, "I will never leave thee, nor forsake thee," let it sink into our hearts as a promise we can hold onto, a reminder that no matter where we go, no matter what we face, we are loved and we are never alone. His voice of faithfulness is the anchor that keeps us steady, the light that guides us forward, and the love that surrounds us always.

Chapter 15 - Slow to Anger Voice

The Shepherd's voice is a voice that is slow to anger, a voice filled with patience, understanding, and kindness, even when we stumble, doubt, or take longer than we should to understand. When we hear that "the Lord is not slack concerning his promise, as some men count slackness; but is longsuffering," we're being reminded of a love that doesn't give up on us, even when we might feel undeserving or think that we've gone too far off track. Imagine the kind of patience it takes to stand by someone through all their mistakes, fears, and hesitations, never losing hope in them, never walking away, and always being ready to guide them back to a place of peace and purpose. That's the kind of patience and gentleness the Shepherd has toward us. His voice isn't filled with impatience or frustration when we make mistakes or struggle to grow; instead, it's filled with a compassionate understanding that sees our struggles, knows our limitations, and loves us through it all. This voice is like the steady presence of a friend who believes in us even when we doubt ourselves, who stands by us even when we feel lost, and who holds on to us with a love that is constant and true. The Shepherd's patience is an active, vibrant force, one that says, "I see your struggles, and I'm here to help, not to condemn." His voice doesn't rush us to be perfect or demand that we have everything figured out right away. Instead, it gives us the room to grow, the grace to make mistakes, and the support to try again. When we fail, His voice doesn't come down on us with anger or disappointment; it comes with encouragement, reminding us that our journey is one of growth, not instant perfection. His longsuffering nature is a gift, a reminder that we are loved deeply, not because we always get it right but because we are His, and that bond is unbreakable. The Shepherd's voice reassures us that He isn't watching and waiting for us to mess up; He is watching and waiting with open arms, ready to catch us, to guide us, and to help us learn from every step along the way. His voice calls us forward with a patience that never wavers, a kindness that never runs out, and a belief in our potential that doesn't diminish, even when we struggle to see it ourselves. This is the voice of someone who knows us better than anyone else, who sees our heart, our intentions, and our efforts, and who loves us just as we are, while gently encouraging us to keep growing. His patience is like a steady river that flows through our lives, calming our fears, softening our hearts, and helping us to see that we are not defined by our mistakes or limitations but by His love and grace. Even when we feel like we're taking two steps forward and one step back, His voice is there, reminding us that progress is still progress, that growth is a journey, and that He is with us every step of the way. The Shepherd's voice is one that doesn't lose hope in us, even when we falter or doubt ourselves. His longsuffering nature means that He waits with an open heart, a willing spirit, and an endless supply of love, knowing that change often takes time and that growth sometimes comes with setbacks. He doesn't get tired of us, and He doesn't get frustrated when we take longer than expected to learn a lesson or to let go of a fear. Instead, His voice comes with a steady patience that invites us to rest in His understanding, to know that we are safe in His care, and to trust that He isn't leaving us behind or losing faith in us. His voice isn't filled with disappointment or frustration; it's filled with hope, a hope that we can feel deep within us, a hope that tells us we are worth the wait, worth the time, and worth the love He so freely gives. His voice calls us back, again and again, each time we stray, not with harshness but with a gentle persistence that says, "I'm here, and I'm not giving up on you." The Shepherd's patience teaches us that we don't have to rush our growth, that we don't have to fear His disappointment, and that we are free to be honest, open, and vulnerable with Him. His slow-to-anger voice invites us to approach Him just as we are, without fear of judgment or rejection, and to know that we are safe in His love. This voice allows us to find comfort in the journey, to trust that we are growing at the pace that's right for us, and to believe that He sees our heart and understands our struggles. His patience is like a balm for our weary souls, giving us the strength to keep moving forward, to keep trying, and to keep trusting, even when the road is hard. His voice is a reminder that love doesn't give up, that kindness doesn't fade, and that His promises remain true, no matter how long it takes for us to understand or to change. When He speaks, it's not with frustration over our failures but with a steady, calming assurance that He is with us, that He is guiding us, and that His love is bigger than any mistake or setback. His patience teaches us to be kind to ourselves, to let go of the fear of failure, and to trust that we are growing, even when we can't see the full picture. This slow-to-anger voice is a voice that loves us at our own pace, that knows that true change takes time, and that believes in us, even when we're struggling to believe in ourselves. The Shepherd's voice of patience is like a quiet song that plays in the background of our lives, reminding us that we are valued, cherished, and understood. His patience with us is a beautiful testament to His love, showing us that we are not defined by how fast we learn or how quickly we change but by His steady, unfailing love. So when we hear His voice say that He is not slack concerning His promise, but is longsuffering, let it be a comfort, a reassurance that we are loved by Someone who will never give up on us, who will never leave us behind, and who will always, always be there, with a heart full of patience and a voice that encourages us to keep going, to keep growing, and to keep trusting in His love. His voice of patience is a gift, a promise, and a constant reminder that we are never alone, and that we are always loved, every step of the way.

Chapter 16 - Sound Voice of Wisdom

The Shepherd's voice is a sound voice of wisdom, a voice that doesn't just tell us what to do, but gently guides us, instructs us, and walks with us on every part of our journey. When we hear the words, "I will instruct thee and teach thee in the way which thou shalt go," it's like being given a promise of guidance and care that will never leave us to wander alone or feel lost. Imagine having Someone who knows every path, every turn, and every choice before you, who understands the hopes and fears in your heart, and who is deeply invested in helping you make decisions that lead to peace, purpose, and joy. The Shepherd's wisdom is not harsh or demanding; it's a calm, steady voice that speaks with a deep love, helping us to see clearly, make thoughtful choices, and find direction even when the way forward seems confusing. His voice doesn't shout or pressure us; it whispers with a kindness that respects our individual journey and encourages us to seek the truth, to look deeper, and to trust that He knows what is best for us. His wisdom is the kind that meets us right where we are, understanding our strengths and weaknesses, and gently nudging us toward what will ultimately bring us peace. It's a voice that doesn't simply give us answers but teaches us how to find them ourselves, helping us grow, learn, and discover the depths of who we are and what we're capable of. The Shepherd's voice of wisdom is patient, taking the time to show us the way, even when we're unsure or hesitant. His guidance is like a light in the darkness, illuminating the path and giving us the confidence to take one step at a time, knowing we are safe in His care. This is the voice of Someone who has walked every path, who knows every outcome, and who is dedicated to leading us in ways that bring us life, love, and fulfillment. The Shepherd doesn't rush us or push us beyond what we're ready for; instead, He teaches us at a pace that we can handle, knowing that true wisdom takes time to grow in our hearts. His instruction isn't just about telling us what to do; it's about shaping us, helping us to become stronger, kinder, and more compassionate. His wisdom encourages us to think for ourselves, to seek the truth, and to find joy in learning and growing. The Shepherd's voice of wisdom doesn't ignore our questions or dismiss our doubts; instead, it meets them with understanding, offering answers that bring clarity and peace. He knows that life is full of choices and challenges, and He wants us to feel confident, not just in His guidance, but in our ability to make wise decisions with His help. His wisdom is gentle and respectful, never forcing or coercing but always inviting us to listen, to learn, and to grow. He doesn't tell us everything all at once; rather, He reveals things to us as we're ready, knowing that true understanding often comes slowly, through experience, patience, and faith. The Shepherd's voice calls us to trust not just in Him, but in the journey, knowing that each step, each lesson, and each moment of growth is part of His plan for us. His wisdom is a gift, a source of comfort and strength that reminds us that we are not alone, that we are guided by a love that is wise, compassionate, and endlessly patient. His instruction is like a compass, helping us to navigate the twists and turns of life with a sense of peace and purpose. He doesn't let us wander aimlessly; He leads us intentionally, with a vision for our lives that is filled with hope, joy, and meaning. His voice of wisdom calls us to pause, to reflect, and to seek understanding, encouraging us to look beyond the surface and to trust in the deeper truths He reveals. The Shepherd doesn't just care about where we're going; He cares about who we are becoming along the way. His wisdom shapes our hearts, our minds, and our spirits, helping us to grow into the people we were created to be. His voice of wisdom reminds us that we don't have to have all the answers, that it's okay to be unsure, and that we are allowed to take our time, to learn, and to grow. He is patient with us, understanding that wisdom is not gained overnight, but through life's experiences, through mistakes, and through the lessons learned along the way. His voice encourages us to keep going, to keep seeking, and to trust that He is with us, guiding us every step of the way. The Shepherd's wisdom is a steady presence, a source of light that leads us through the uncertainties of life, reminding us that we are not alone, that we are cared for, and that we are always loved. His instruction is not about control but about freedom, a freedom that comes from knowing that we are on the right path, that we are guided by Someone who knows and loves us deeply. This is a voice that calls us to be courageous, to seek the truth, and to find joy in the journey, knowing that we are held in the hands of a Shepherd who is wise, kind, and faithful. His wisdom is a gift that gives us strength, hope, and the assurance that we are never left to face life on our own. So when we hear His voice say, "I will instruct thee and teach thee in the way which thou shalt go," let it be a comfort, a reminder that we are loved, guided, and held by a wisdom that will never fail us. His voice of wisdom is a constant, a blessing, and a promise that we are never alone, that we are always being led by a love that is perfect, and that we are safe in the care of a Shepherd who will never lead us astray.

Chapter 17 - Straightforward Voice of Justice

The Shepherd's voice is a straightforward voice of justice, a voice that speaks clearly, honestly, and firmly about what is right and true. When we hear that "the Lord is righteous, he loveth righteousness," we are reminded that His love for us is rooted in a deep sense of justice, fairness, and truth. Imagine knowing that there is Someone who sees everything—the good, the bad, the hidden struggles, and the overlooked acts of kindness—and who loves what is right and good with a passion that never fades. The Shepherd's voice of justice is not harsh or condemning; it is a voice that cares deeply about every person, every action, and every decision, and it calls us to live in a way that reflects His love for what is true and just. His voice is like a light in the darkness, revealing what is good, encouraging us to do what is right, and helping us to understand the importance of fairness and kindness in all we do. This is not a voice that makes us feel judged or condemned; instead, it is a voice that inspires us to strive for integrity, to stand up for what is right, and to care for those around us with compassion and respect. The Shepherd's justice is pure, free from selfishness or bias, and it shows us the beauty of living a life that honors both God and others. His straightforward voice of justice reminds us that we are called to be people of character, to act with honesty, and to treat others with dignity. He loves righteousness because it reflects His own character—strong, pure, and full of love. When He speaks to us about justice, it is not to intimidate or control but to guide us toward a life that is full of peace, fairness, and respect. His voice tells us that every person has worth, that every act of kindness matters, and that each time we choose to do what is right, we are reflecting His love in the world. The Shepherd's justice is not about punishment but about setting things right, about bringing peace to situations of conflict and hope to places of despair. His voice of justice calls us to look beyond ourselves, to see the needs of others, and to act with a heart that values fairness, truth, and compassion. He does not love righteousness in a distant or abstract way; He loves it because He knows that justice and truth bring healing, hope, and peace to our lives. His straightforward voice encourages us to be people who care for others, who stand up for what is right, and who live in a way that brings light and goodness into the world. The Shepherd's justice is not about rigid rules or impossible standards; it's about living with integrity, about making choices that honor God and uplift others. His voice of justice is a reminder that we are called to do more than just avoid wrong; we are called to actively seek out ways to bring kindness, fairness, and love into the world. The Shepherd loves righteousness because it is the foundation of a life that is good, peaceful, and filled with respect for all people. His voice speaks to our hearts, showing us that we don't have to be perfect, but we are invited to grow, to learn, and to live with a purpose that reflects His own love for justice. This is a voice that calls us to honesty, to fairness, and to a life that shines with the goodness of God. It reminds us that justice is not just a concept; it's a way of life that honors others and brings us closer to the Shepherd. His straightforward voice of justice does not condemn us for our mistakes; instead, it calls us to rise above them, to seek forgiveness, and to make choices that are true to His love for what is right. The Shepherd's justice is a guiding light, a clear and steady voice that shows us the path of goodness, fairness, and love. His love for righteousness is not a burden or a demand; it is an invitation to live in a way that brings peace to our hearts and joy to those around us. His voice encourages us to seek justice in our lives, to stand up for those who are hurting, and to live with a kindness that reflects His own compassionate heart. The Shepherd's voice is one of encouragement, one that inspires us to be better, to love deeper, and to make a difference in the lives of others. His love for justice is part of His love for us, a love that wants the best for each person and the world as a whole. His straightforward voice of justice reminds us that we are capable of making choices that bring goodness into the world, that we have the power to impact others with fairness and kindness. This is not a voice of condemnation but a voice of hope, a voice that believes in our ability to live with integrity and love. The Shepherd's justice is a beautiful thing, a voice that calls us to live honestly, to treat others with respect, and to stand up for what is right, even when it's difficult. His love for righteousness is not about following a list of rules; it's about becoming the kind of people who bring love, peace, and fairness into every situation. The

Shepherd's voice of justice is a promise that He is with us, guiding us to live lives that reflect His love and honor His truth. His straightforward voice encourages us to live with courage, to speak the truth in love, and to act with kindness and integrity. He does not expect us to be perfect, but He does invite us to walk with Him, to learn from Him, and to grow in His love for what is right and just. His justice is not a distant or cold concept; it is a warm, inviting call to live in a way that makes a positive impact on the lives of others. The Shepherd's voice of justice is a constant reminder that we are valued, that we are loved, and that we have a purpose in this world. His love for righteousness is a reminder that we are called to be lights in the world, to bring peace to conflict, and to show kindness to those who need it most. His straightforward voice of justice is not a harsh demand but a gentle invitation to live a life that is filled with purpose, love, and respect for all people. So when we hear His voice, calling us to seek justice and to love righteousness, let it remind us that we are not alone, that we are guided by a Shepherd who loves us deeply, and that we have the power to make a difference in the world with kindness, fairness, and love. His voice of justice is a gift, a blessing, and a promise that we are never alone and that we are always loved by a Shepherd who is righteous, compassionate, and true.

Chapter 18 - Strong Voice of Power

The Shepherd's voice is a strong voice of power, a voice that speaks with authority, clarity, and an unmatched strength that can reach right into the deepest parts of our hearts and lives. When we hear that "the word of God is quick, and powerful, and sharper than any two-edged sword," it's a reminder that His voice isn't just comforting or kind—it's also mighty, able to cut through the noise, confusion, and chaos of life to bring truth, clarity, and direction. This voice of power is a source of strength and guidance in times when we feel uncertain or when we face challenges that seem bigger than we can handle. Imagine a voice that knows exactly what needs to be said, that speaks with a force that commands attention, not because it's loud or overwhelming but because it's true and unwavering. The Shepherd's voice is like a light that pierces through darkness, a powerful truth that breaks through our fears and doubts, reminding us of what really matters and where we should stand. His words don't simply comfort us; they empower us, giving us the courage to face life's battles, to stand strong, and to keep moving forward, even when the path is hard. This powerful voice doesn't just tell us what we want to hear; it tells us what we need to know, speaking directly to our hearts with a wisdom that sees beyond our limited perspective. The Shepherd's voice is strong and precise, like a two-edged sword that cuts away our fears, our worries, and our misunderstandings, bringing us closer to the truth of who we are and who we are called to be. His words are alive, filled with energy and purpose, reaching deep into our souls to ignite a strength we may not have even known we had. The Shepherd speaks to us with a voice that doesn't falter, a voice that doesn't back down, a voice that knows the power of truth and uses it to protect, to guide, and to uplift us. This isn't a voice that leaves us feeling weak or afraid; it's a voice that strengthens us, reminding us that we are capable, that we are loved, and that we are never alone. His powerful voice is like a fortress around us, a shield that guards us from lies and discouragement, filling us with a confidence that comes from knowing we are held by Someone infinitely strong and endlessly faithful. The Shepherd's words are powerful because they come from a place of deep understanding and love, and they are meant to build us up, to encourage us, and to give us a firm foundation to stand on. When He speaks, His voice has the power to calm storms within us, to heal our brokenness, and to fill us with a peace that nothing else can provide. His words cut through our doubts, reminding us of who we are and whose we are, grounding us in a love that is unbreakable and a truth that is eternal. The strength of His voice doesn't come from force or intimidation; it comes from a pure, unwavering love that wants the very best for us. He speaks to us with a power that challenges us to rise above our fears, to embrace the truth, and to walk boldly in the path He has set for us. His words don't leave us feeling small or inadequate; they lift us up, calling us to see ourselves as He sees us—strong, loved, and capable of great things. The Shepherd's voice is not only strong but also deeply compassionate, using His power not to control us but to free us from the things that hold us back. His powerful words cut away the lies we sometimes believe about ourselves, about others, or about what's possible. His voice brings clarity, helping us to see past our fears and to recognize the strength He has placed within us. This isn't a power that seeks to dominate; it's a power that seeks to protect, to uplift, and to encourage. The Shepherd's voice reminds us that we don't have to be strong on our own, that His strength is there for us, ready to support us in every challenge we face. His voice is like a rock we can stand on, a firm foundation that holds us steady, no matter what storms come our way. The power of His words is a reminder that we are not alone, that we have a Shepherd who is strong enough to carry us, to guide us, and to defend us in every situation. His words aren't just inspiring; they are transforming, giving us the courage to become who we are meant to be. When the Shepherd speaks, His voice is a reminder that we are loved by a power greater than anything we can face, that we are protected by a strength that never wavers, and that we are guided by a wisdom that knows the way forward, even when we don't. His powerful words don't just lift us up; they ground us in a truth that gives us purpose, direction, and peace. The Shepherd's voice isn't harsh or frightening; it's a voice of love, a love so strong that it refuses to let us settle for anything less than the truth and the fullness of life He has for us. His powerful words don't leave us feeling weighed down; they set us free, freeing us from fear, doubt, and anything else that tries to hold us back. His voice tells us that we are strong, not because of anything we've done, but because He is with us, guiding us, strengthening us, and speaking truth into our lives. The power of His words is like a light that breaks through the darkness, giving us the courage to face each day with hope, to walk forward with confidence, and to trust that we are being led by Someone who knows and loves us completely. The Shepherd's voice of power is a gift, a blessing, and a constant reminder that we are held, loved, and guided by a strength that is unshakable and a truth that is unbreakable. So when we hear His voice, let it remind us that we are never alone, that we are deeply loved, and that we are always held in the powerful, loving hands of the Shepherd who calls us His own. His voice is strong, His love is constant, and His guidance is a light that will never fade.

Chapter 19 - Sweet Voice of Mercy

The Shepherd's voice is a sweet voice of mercy, a voice that calls us with kindness and understanding, inviting us to come close, to let go of our burdens, and to find forgiveness and peace. When He says, "Come now, and let us reason together," He's offering us a chance to bring everything we carry—our mistakes, our regrets, our fears—and lay them down without fear of rejection. Imagine being welcomed with open arms, not judged or condemned, but accepted fully, knowing that every fault and flaw is already known and yet completely forgiven. This is what the Shepherd's mercy feels like, a gentle and sweet invitation to leave behind the weight of guilt and to find a fresh start, a clean slate, where even our worst moments are not held against us. His voice of mercy tells us that, though our sins may feel like a stain we can't wash away, in His love, they are removed, made as white as snow. It's like having a deep, painful scar that we try to cover, hoping no one sees it, only to find that the Shepherd knows all about it and still reaches out to heal it. His mercy is a balm for our souls, giving us the courage to face the parts of ourselves we may be ashamed of, the mistakes we try to hide, and the regrets that haunt us. He doesn't turn away from our weaknesses or our failures; instead, He draws near, gently assuring us that His love is greater than any wrong we have done. The sweetness of His mercy is that it doesn't ask us to be perfect; it simply asks us to come, to be real, to let down our defenses, and to trust that we are loved just as we are. His voice is soft yet powerful, telling us that forgiveness isn't something we have to earn but something He freely gives because He loves us that deeply. His mercy is a gift, a second chance, a new beginning that lets us step out of the shadows of shame and into the light of His grace. The Shepherd's mercy is not a one-time offer; it's a constant, always waiting for us, always available, no matter how many times we stumble. His voice says, "Come, let us reason together," as if He's saying, "Let's sit down and talk, let's face this together, and let Me carry the weight you feel." He doesn't rush us or push us to change faster than we're able; He meets us where we are, gently guiding us toward healing, toward peace, and toward a life that is no longer chained to our past mistakes. His mercy is like a river, flowing freely, washing over us, making us new, and reminding us that we are more than our failures. In His mercy, there is a sweetness, a kindness that wraps around us, helping us to believe that we are worth loving, that we are worth forgiving, and that we are worth redeeming. The Shepherd's voice doesn't bring up our wrongs to make us feel guilty; instead, He calls them to light only to lift them from us, to assure us that we don't have to carry that burden anymore. His mercy is patient, understanding that we may need time to forgive ourselves even as He has already forgiven us. His voice is a constant reminder that no sin, no mistake, no regret is too great for His love to cover. The sweet mercy in His voice tells us that we are free to leave the past behind, to let go of the things that weigh us down, and to live a life filled with hope, peace, and joy. His mercy is not only sweet but powerful, transforming us from the inside out, helping us to see ourselves through His eyes—not as failures or sinners but as beloved children who are worth every ounce of His love and grace. This voice of mercy calls us to a life where we don't have to hide or pretend; we are free to be ourselves, knowing that we are fully accepted. His mercy is like a gentle rain that washes away the dust, refreshing us, renewing us, and making us feel whole again. He doesn't remind us of our past to shame us; He speaks of forgiveness to free us, to release us from any sense of unworthiness, and to show us that we are, indeed, loved beyond measure. The sweetness of His mercy invites us to trust, to believe that, no matter where we've been or what we've done, there is always a way forward, always a chance for healing, and always hope for a better tomorrow. The Shepherd's mercy is a safe place, a refuge where we can come with our fears, our doubts, and our deepest regrets, and know that we are still loved, still wanted, and still cherished. His voice calls us not just to be forgiven but to be renewed, to live with a light heart, and to know that we are not defined by our sins but by His love for us. This sweet voice of mercy is a promise that we don't have to walk alone, that every misstep, every failure is met with compassion and a willingness to help us rise again. His mercy is an invitation to live in the freedom of forgiveness, to let go of the chains that bind us, and to embrace the life He has for us, a life filled with purpose, peace, and unending love. So when we hear His voice, saying, "Come now, let us reason together," let it remind us that we are not too broken, not too lost, and not too far gone. His mercy reaches us wherever we are, lifting us up, holding us close, and assuring us that we are His, forever loved and forever forgiven.

Chapter 20 - Saving Voice of Forgiveness

The Shepherd's voice is a saving voice of forgiveness, a voice that doesn't condemn or push us away for our mistakes but instead reaches out with a mercy that is both powerful and gentle, saying, "Neither do I condemn thee: go, and sin no more." These words aren't just a simple statement; they're a lifeline, a promise, and a gift of new beginnings, showing us that no matter what we've done or where we've been, we are offered forgiveness and a fresh start. Imagine being caught in a moment where you feel all your flaws and mistakes are on display, the kind of moment where shame and regret weigh heavily on your heart. In that moment, rather than turning away or pointing a finger, the Shepherd comes close, looks you in the eye, and says these beautiful words of grace and kindness: "I do not condemn you." It's as if He's taking the weight of guilt off your shoulders, giving you permission to release the burdens you've been carrying, and reminding you that your mistakes don't define you in His eyes. This voice of forgiveness is freeing, healing, and filled with a love that sees beyond our flaws, reaching deep into our hearts and helping us understand that we are more than our worst moments. He doesn't brush aside our actions as if they don't matter; instead, He offers us a chance to rise above them, to be better, to learn, and to move forward with a renewed spirit. His forgiveness is like a bridge that helps us cross from a place of shame and regret to a place of peace, hope, and self-acceptance. When He says, "Go, and sin no more," it's not a harsh command but a gentle invitation to live differently, to embrace a life that is free from the chains of past mistakes, and to trust that with His guidance, we can walk a path that brings us joy and fulfillment. The Shepherd's voice doesn't linger on what we did wrong; instead, it points us toward what we can do right from here on out. He knows that we are human, that we will stumble, and that sometimes we will make poor choices, but His forgiveness is always ready to catch us, to pull us back up, and to give us another chance. This saving voice of forgiveness is like a soft whisper in a world that often shouts about failure and judgment. It's a quiet but powerful reminder that mercy is stronger than punishment, and that love is greater than any mistake we could make. He looks beyond our faults and sees our potential, focusing not on where we've failed but on where we're going. His forgiveness isn't just about wiping the slate clean; it's about giving us the strength and courage to keep going, to try again, and to live in a way that reflects the love He has shown us. When we hear Him say, "Neither do I condemn you," it's like a light breaking through darkness, a breath of fresh air that tells us it's okay to let go of the past, to forgive ourselves, and to embrace the life that He has planned for us. His voice of forgiveness teaches us that we don't have to live in guilt, that we don't have to be trapped by our mistakes, and that we have the power to change, to grow, and to be better. This saving voice calls us out of shame and into freedom, out of regret and into hope, out of self-doubt and into a new sense of purpose. The Shepherd's forgiveness is not given with reluctance or hesitation; it is given freely, fully, and with a heart that wants nothing more than to see us happy, whole, and at peace. He understands our struggles, our fears, and our regrets, and He meets us right where we are, offering a love that doesn't hold grudges or keep score. His forgiveness is a gift that we don't have to earn or prove ourselves worthy of; it's a gift that is given simply because we are His, and He loves us beyond measure. When He says, "Go, and sin no more," He is calling us to live in the light of His love, to leave behind the things that weigh us down, and to step into a future that is filled with hope, purpose, and joy. His voice doesn't condemn or criticize; it encourages, uplifts, and gently guides us toward a better way of living. The Shepherd's forgiveness is a chance to start fresh, to rebuild, and to know that we are not defined by our past. It is a promise that we are always given another chance, that we are never too far gone, and that we are forever loved. His voice of forgiveness is like a safe place where we can be honest, open, and unafraid of rejection. It's a voice that tells us we don't have to hide our flaws or pretend to be perfect; instead, we can come as we are, knowing that His love covers everything we could ever regret. This saving voice is a reminder that every day is a new opportunity, a new chance to walk in the love and grace He offers so freely. His forgiveness doesn't ignore our mistakes; it transforms them, using them as stepping stones to help us grow, learn, and become the people we were always meant to be. When we feel lost, ashamed, or unworthy, His voice is there to remind us that we are His beloved, that we are forgiven, and that we are cherished just as we are. The Shepherd's voice of forgiveness is a call to freedom, a release from the chains of guilt and shame, and an invitation to live a life that is full of hope, joy, and love. It's a voice that doesn't give up on us, no matter how many times we fall or how far we wander. His forgiveness is endless, always ready, always available, and always given with a heart full of compassion. So when we hear Him say, "Neither do I condemn thee," let it be a reminder that we are not alone, that we are loved beyond measure, and that we have a place in His heart forever. His saving voice of forgiveness is a blessing, a promise, and a beautiful truth that we can carry with us always, knowing that we are forgiven, we are loved, and we are free.

Chapter 21 - Soft Voice of Gentleness

The Shepherd's voice is a soft voice of gentleness, a voice that tenderly cares for us, just as a shepherd would carefully feed and gather his flock, gently holding each lamb close. When we hear, "He shall feed his flock like a shepherd: he shall gather the lambs with his arm," it paints a picture of the loving care and attention He gives to each of us. Imagine the safety of being held in such loving arms, arms that don't let go, arms that carry you when you're tired, hurt, or simply need rest. This gentle voice of the Shepherd is unlike any other; it speaks softly to our hearts, inviting us to let down our guard and trust that we are cared for in ways we can hardly imagine. His voice doesn't push or force; it simply calls, like a soothing melody that wraps around us, telling us it's safe to be ourselves, to bring all our fears, worries, and needs before Him without fear of rejection or disappointment. This gentleness is a strength, a kind of power that doesn't need to shout or demand because it is grounded in a love that is deep, faithful, and constant. The Shepherd's voice is gentle enough to reach even the most fragile places in us, places we may try to hide from others or even from ourselves. He understands our struggles, our weariness, and the parts of us that feel vulnerable, and He speaks to these places with a care that reassures us that we are not alone. His voice is like a quiet stream, calming the storms within us, bringing peace to our restless hearts, and reminding us that we are loved just as we are. The gentleness of His voice tells us that we don't have to be perfect or have everything figured out; we only need to come to Him, and He will provide for us, feed us, and hold us close. Just as a shepherd knows each of his sheep, the Lord knows each of us intimately, knowing what we need even before we ask. His voice speaks directly to our hearts, filling us with a sense of worth and belonging that the world often fails to give. His voice doesn't judge or criticize; instead, it lifts us up, helping us see ourselves as He sees us—precious, beloved, and valuable. The Shepherd's gentleness is a reminder that we are safe in His care, that we have a place of refuge where we are accepted unconditionally. When we feel weak or overwhelmed, His soft voice encourages us, telling us that we don't have to carry our burdens alone. He is there to help, to comfort, and to guide us, gently gathering us like a shepherd gathers his lambs, close to His heart, where we are protected and cherished. His voice of gentleness is not distant or abstract; it is personal, tender, and compassionate, meeting us exactly where we are. In a world that often seems harsh or demanding, His gentle voice is a balm to our souls, a quiet reminder that we are loved, that we are seen, and that we are held by a love that never fades. His gentleness doesn't mean weakness; it is a strength that comes from a heart full of love, a love that chooses to be kind, to be patient, and to care for us with a dedication that is unchanging. This voice calls us back to a place of peace, where we can rest and find new strength, knowing that we are not alone. The Shepherd's gentleness teaches us to be kind to ourselves, to forgive our own mistakes, and to approach life with a heart open to love and compassion. His voice is a guide, a protector, and a comforter, gently leading us to green pastures, to quiet waters, and to the safety of His care. He doesn't rush us or demand that we move faster than we're able; instead, He matches our pace, walking with us through every moment, every struggle, and every joy. His gentle voice is always there, a constant source of encouragement that fills us with hope, reminding us that we are never too far, never too broken, and never beyond the reach of His love. His voice tells us that we are worth caring for, worth holding close, and worth every moment of His attention. The Shepherd's gentleness is a gift, a love that doesn't change with our mistakes or fade with our doubts; it remains, steady and true, always ready to comfort and support us. So when we hear His soft voice, calling us like a shepherd calls his lambs, let it remind us that we are precious, that we are loved, and that we have a place in His arms, where we are forever safe and forever cherished. His voice of gentleness is our refuge, our comfort, and our peace, a reminder that no matter where we are or what we face, we are always, always held close by the Shepherd who loves us beyond measure.

Chapter 22 - Sure Voice of Unchanging Nature

The Shepherd's voice is a sure voice of unchanging nature, a voice that is steady, reliable, and eternally faithful, speaking with a promise that cannot be broken: "For I am the Lord, I change not." These words bring a peace to our hearts like nothing else can, reminding us that in a world filled with change, uncertainty, and things that can often feel so unpredictable, we have Someone we can always count on, Someone whose love and promises are as constant as the stars in the sky. Imagine a love that never fades, a commitment that never wavers, and a promise that stands strong no matter what storms life may bring. This is the Shepherd's unchanging nature, a foundation of steadfastness that tells us we are safe, that we are loved, and that we have nothing to fear because He is always the same. His voice doesn't shift with the trends, doesn't falter in tough times, and doesn't grow tired of us. Instead, His love remains as strong and as real today as it was yesterday, and as it will be tomorrow and forever. His voice is a comfort when we feel lost or alone, reminding us that, while people or circumstances in life may disappoint or change unexpectedly, He will never change. His promises are dependable, His love is unwavering, and His presence is always near, ready to support us through whatever we're going through. This unchanging voice of the Shepherd reassures us that no matter what changes around us, no matter how much we feel uncertain or afraid, we are held in the hands of a God who never shifts or wavers in His care for us. His unchanging nature is like a rock that we can lean on, a shelter that stands strong in the storm, a refuge that is always open and always safe. In a world where so much is temporary and fragile, His voice is a reminder that we have something eternal, something solid and true that will never break or leave us. This voice of unchanging love tells us that we don't have to worry about ever being abandoned, forgotten, or left behind. His unchanging nature means that His promises stay the same; they are just as real and powerful today as they were when they were first spoken. His voice reminds us that His commitment to us doesn't depend on our circumstances, on our actions, or even on our feelings. He is with us in every season of life, through every joy and sorrow, remaining as loving and faithful as He has always been. His love doesn't fade when we make mistakes or lose our way; instead, His voice calls us back with the same kindness, the same patience, and the same hope that He's always had for us. This unchanging nature of the Shepherd is a gift, a reassurance that we can trust Him completely, that we can bring our fears, our dreams, and our doubts to Him, knowing that He will meet us with the same unshakable love every time. When life feels overwhelming, His steady voice is there, grounding us, reminding us that we are held by a love that doesn't change. His words are not like the promises of this world that can be broken or forgotten; they are eternal, strong, and true, offering us a hope that doesn't disappoint. His unchanging voice tells us that we don't have to be afraid of the future or anxious about the unknown because we have a Shepherd who will be with us through every change, every transition, every moment. His constancy brings us a deep sense of peace, knowing that even when everything else shifts, He is a constant presence, a loving guide, and a faithful friend. His voice doesn't depend on how good or bad we are, how successful or how flawed we may feel; it simply depends on His own unchanging love, a love that remains no matter what. His unchanging nature tells us that His kindness, His grace, and His forgiveness are always available, ready to lift us up, to guide us, and to fill us with a peace that the world cannot offer. His voice is a gentle but powerful reminder that we are safe in His love, that we are treasured beyond measure, and that we are held by a Shepherd who will never let us go. His promises are not empty words; they are lifelines, truths that we can cling to, knowing that He is faithful to fulfill them. This unchanging voice of the Shepherd gives us confidence, strength, and hope, helping us to stand firm even when everything around us feels unstable or uncertain. We can rest in His unchanging nature, knowing that His love for us is as real and as strong as it has always been. His voice assures us that we are never alone, that we are never forgotten, and that we are always loved. The Shepherd's unchanging voice is a gift that gives us security and peace, allowing us to walk through life with courage, knowing that we are anchored in a love that will never fail. So when we hear His voice say, "I change not," let it remind us that we are held by the One who is forever faithful, forever loving, and forever ours. His unchanging voice is a blessing, a promise, and a constant light that guides us, comforts us, and reminds us that we are safe in His care, now and always.

Chapter 23 - Searching Voice of Conviction

The Shepherd's voice is a searching voice of conviction, a voice that lovingly reaches out to the depths of our hearts, not to condemn or accuse but to gently call us toward honesty, healing, and forgiveness. When we hear, "If we confess our sins, he is faithful and just to forgive us our sins," we're being invited into a moment of truth, a safe space where we can come just as we are, with all our mistakes, regrets, and hidden faults. This isn't a voice that points fingers or shames us; it's a voice that seeks to bring us closer, to free us from the burdens we often try to carry alone. Imagine the peace of being able to open up completely, to be vulnerable, and to know that you're not going to be rejected or judged. The Shepherd's voice speaks with a compassion that sees everything about us—the good, the flawed, and the broken—and still calls us His beloved. His voice of conviction is a voice that encourages us to be honest, not because He wants us to feel bad about ourselves but because He wants to help us let go of the things that weigh down our hearts and hold us back from living fully. This voice searches our hearts gently, like a caring friend who wants the best for us, helping us to see the things we need to bring into the light, not to condemn but to heal. He knows that carrying around guilt, shame, and hidden burdens only keeps us feeling trapped and alone, so His voice calls us to confess, to open up, and to let His forgiveness wash over us like a gentle rain, cleansing us and setting us free. The Shepherd's voice doesn't force or demand; it simply invites, reaching out with a kindness that makes us feel safe, a love that tells us it's okay to be real, and a grace that reminds us that we don't have to be perfect to be loved. This searching voice of conviction is about giving us the courage to face the parts of ourselves we may not want to look at, the mistakes we regret, and the flaws we try to hide. He calls us not to be perfect but to be honest, promising that His love is big enough to hold all our messes, all our doubts, and all our fears. His voice is steady, calming, and filled with a warmth that lets us know we are not alone, that we don't have to carry our guilt on our own shoulders because He is ready to lift it from us. When we confess, it's like taking off a heavy backpack we've been carrying for too long, a backpack filled with things that were never meant to be carried alone. The Shepherd's voice of conviction is here to help us unload that weight, to bring it all to Him, and to trust that His forgiveness is ready and waiting, just as constant and true as His love. He doesn't hold grudges or keep a record of our wrongs; instead, He promises that if we come to Him, confessing the things that trouble our hearts, He is faithful and just, ready to forgive without hesitation. This is not a conditional love that depends on us being flawless; it's an unconditional love that simply asks us to come as we are, to be open, and to let go of the things that no longer serve us. His voice of conviction isn't harsh or punishing; it's freeing, a reminder that we don't have to live in the shadows of guilt or hide in the dark corners of shame. His forgiveness is like a fresh start, a clean slate that tells us we are more than our mistakes, that we are loved beyond our faults, and that we have a Shepherd who is willing to walk with us every step of the way. His searching voice encourages us to live in the light, to be honest with ourselves and with Him, and to trust that His forgiveness is always within reach. This voice doesn't shame us for our past; it gives us hope for our future, reminding us that no matter how far we've strayed, there is always a way back. The Shepherd's voice of conviction is like a gentle hand reaching out, inviting us to let go of the things that burden us, the fears that hold us back, and the regrets that weigh heavy on our hearts. His forgiveness is not something we have to earn or prove ourselves worthy of; it's a gift, a constant that is always there, waiting for us to come close, to open up, and to receive the peace He offers. His searching voice is a comfort, a promise that we are never alone, and that we are always welcomed back into His arms, no matter where we've been or what we've done. His forgiveness is faithful and just, a promise that doesn't change with our circumstances or depend on our worthiness. This voice of conviction calls us to step into the light, to embrace the freedom of being fully known and fully loved, and to trust that we are held by a love that is greater than any mistake we could ever make. The Shepherd's voice of conviction is a call to honesty, a reminder that we are safe in His love, and a reassurance that His forgiveness is always within reach.

Chapter 24 - Sustaining Voice of Comfort

The Shepherd's voice is a sustaining voice of comfort, a voice that speaks to the very core of our tired and burdened souls, saying, "Cast thy burden upon the Lord, and he shall sustain thee." It's a voice that invites us to let go of the weight we carry, to release all the worries, fears, and struggles that have become too heavy to bear alone. Imagine the relief of being told you don't have to carry it all on your own, that there is Someone who sees every burden, understands every worry, and is waiting with open arms to take it from you, to share the load, and to give you the strength you need. This is what the Shepherd's sustaining voice offers—a place to lay down what's too much, a place of peace where we don't have to hold everything together by ourselves. His voice doesn't push or force; it simply calls gently, inviting us to trust that we are not alone, that there is help, comfort, and rest waiting for us if we are willing to let go. He doesn't ask us to pretend that everything is okay or to hide our struggles; He knows every tear, every worry, every doubt, and He loves us just the same. His sustaining voice tells us it's okay to be tired, it's okay to need rest, and it's okay to rely on Him. In a world that often tells us to be strong, to push through, and to never show weakness, the Shepherd's voice is a breath of fresh air, a reminder that we don't have to be strong all the time, that we are allowed to lean on Him, to let Him carry what feels too heavy. His voice of comfort is steady and reassuring, reminding us that He is with us in every moment, in every struggle, and that He will never let us fall. This sustaining voice doesn't just offer temporary relief; it offers a deep, lasting peace, a sense that no matter what we face, we are held by a love that is constant, powerful, and infinitely compassionate. The Shepherd's voice is like a gentle hand reaching out to us, a soft invitation to release the burdens we've been carrying, to trust that we don't have to walk this path alone. His comfort isn't a vague feeling; it's a solid, unshakable support that lifts us up when we're weary, that fills us with hope when we're discouraged, and that reminds us we are cherished and valued, no matter what. His sustaining voice is a constant presence, a voice that tells us we are safe, we are loved, and we are supported, even in the hardest times. When He says, "Cast thy burden upon me," He is saying that we don't have to be everything, that we don't have to hold all the answers, and that we don't have to solve every problem on our own. His voice of comfort is a reminder that we are not meant to carry everything by ourselves, that we have a Shepherd who is strong enough, loving enough, and faithful enough to hold us and all of our worries, no matter how big or small. The Shepherd's sustaining voice encourages us to be honest about our struggles, to bring our fears, our doubts, and our pain to Him, knowing that He is there to help us through. His comfort is like a warm embrace, a place where we can breathe easy, knowing that we are understood, that we are seen, and that we are loved exactly as we are. His voice doesn't judge us for feeling overwhelmed; instead, it reassures us that it's okay, that He is with us, and that His strength is there to fill in where ours runs out. The sustaining comfort of His voice tells us that we are not weak for needing help, that we are not alone in our struggles, and that we are deeply cherished, even when we feel broken or lost. His voice is a constant support, a reminder that we can lean on Him, that we can let go of what feels too heavy, and that we can trust that He will provide the strength, peace, and comfort we need. His sustaining voice is always there, calling us to rest, to let go, and to find peace in His unchanging love. In moments when we feel like we can't take another step, His voice is there, gently encouraging us, lifting us up, and helping us to see that we are never truly alone. The Shepherd's comfort is not fleeting; it is a steady presence, a reminder that we are held, that we are supported, and that we are loved beyond measure. So when we hear His voice say, "Cast thy burden upon the Lord," let it be a reminder that we are not alone, that we are deeply loved, and that we are always, always sustained by the Shepherd who cares for us with a love that is infinite, gentle, and strong. His voice of comfort is our refuge, our strength, and our peace, a constant reminder that no matter what we face, we are never alone.

Chapter 25 - Stirring Voice of Hope

The Shepherd's voice is a stirring voice of hope, a voice that reaches out to us with a promise that we are never alone, saying, "I am with you alway, even unto the end of the world." This is not just a comforting phrase; it's a profound commitment, a declaration of presence that wraps around us like a warm, steady embrace, especially in those moments when we feel lost, overwhelmed, or unsure of what lies ahead. Imagine the peace that comes from knowing, with absolute certainty, that there is Someone who will stand by your side through every season, every challenge, and every joy in your life. The Shepherd's voice stirs hope within us, not because it promises an easy life, but because it promises a constant, faithful presence that will not waver or disappear when things get tough. This voice is like a light in the darkness, a steady hand that guides us when the path seems unclear and reminds us that we are loved deeply and seen fully, no matter what. The Shepherd's voice of hope doesn't deny that life has its difficulties; it acknowledges our pain, our doubts, and our fears, yet speaks into them with a calm assurance that we do not walk this journey alone. His presence is not conditional; it's a promise that doesn't depend on our actions or circumstances but on His unchanging love for us. When we face situations that feel overwhelming or too heavy to carry, His voice whispers to our hearts, reminding us that He is with us, giving us the courage to face each day, each step, and each moment. The Shepherd doesn't abandon us when we falter or struggle; instead, He draws closer, offering His strength when we feel weak, His peace when we feel anxious, and His hope when we feel uncertain. His voice is like a quiet, unbreakable thread of hope woven into every part of our lives, telling us that no matter how far we wander, how many mistakes we make, or how alone we may feel, He is always there. His presence is like a strong foundation under our feet, a place we can return to again and again, knowing that we are welcomed, loved, and cherished. The Shepherd's voice stirs a hope that reaches beyond our circumstances, a hope that doesn't depend on what is happening around us but is rooted in the assurance that He is with us, holding us, guiding us, and loving us with a love that never ends. This voice of hope calls us to lift our eyes, to look beyond our immediate struggles, and to trust that there is a bigger picture, a greater story in which we are deeply valued and purposefully placed. Even when we can't see what's ahead or don't understand why things happen, His voice reminds us that we are safe in His care, that we are part of something beautiful, and that we are held in hands that will never let us go. The Shepherd's voice isn't just a promise of presence; it's a reminder of our worth, our purpose, and the unshakable fact that we are loved beyond measure. His words are like a gentle but powerful reminder that we are never abandoned, that we are never out of His reach, and that we are always seen, always known, and always treasured. This hope stirs within us the courage to keep going, to trust, and to rest in the knowledge that we have a constant Companion who sees every part of us, who knows our fears, our dreams, and our desires, and who will be with us through every moment of our lives. His voice of hope is steady and reassuring, telling us that even when we face the unknown, even when we walk through valleys of uncertainty, He is right beside us, whispering words of love, strength, and peace. The Shepherd doesn't promise that we will always understand the path or that life will be without struggles; instead, He promises that we will never face those struggles alone. His voice calls us to trust, to believe in His love, and to know that, whatever comes, we are held in a love that is unbreakable, steadfast, and true. His presence gives us the strength to face each day with hope, to rise above our fears, and to find peace in the assurance that we are never alone. When we feel afraid, His voice reminds us that we have nothing to fear; when we feel discouraged, His voice speaks courage into our hearts; and when we feel lost, His voice gently guides us back, showing us that we are always found in His love. The Shepherd's voice of hope is a constant, a promise that stands firm no matter what life brings, a reminder that we are never abandoned and that we are always, always loved. His words call us to live with hope, to trust in His goodness, and to remember that we are part of a story that ends in love, peace, and joy. His voice of hope is a beacon, a steady light that shines in our hearts, giving us the strength to keep going, to keep believing, and to know, with all certainty, that we are not alone. So when we hear His voice, saying, "I am with you alway, even unto the end of the world," let it remind us that we are never alone, that we are deeply loved, and that we are held in the unchanging, ever-faithful embrace of a Shepherd who will never let us go. His voice of hope is our comfort, our strength, and our peace, a constant assurance that we are safe, we are seen, and we are forever loved.

Chapter 26 - Satisfying Voice of Love

The Shepherd's voice is a satisfying voice of love, a voice that speaks to us with a deep, everlasting affection that fills the empty spaces in our hearts and whispers, "Yea, I have loved thee with an everlasting love." This is not just a fleeting feeling or a momentary kindness—it's a love that never fades, a love that reaches into every corner of our lives, meeting us in our joys, our struggles, and our quiet moments of doubt. Imagine a love so complete, so pure, and so constant that nothing you do could ever change it, diminish it, or make it go away. This is the kind of love the Shepherd has for each of us, a love that doesn't depend on our actions, our successes, or our failures. It's a love that exists simply because we are His, because we are cherished, and because we are wanted. His voice of love isn't loud or demanding; it's gentle, patient, and kind, inviting us to come close, to be ourselves, and to know that we are enough just as we are. This satisfying love speaks to the deepest parts of our hearts, reminding us that we are not alone, that we are valued beyond measure, and that we have a place in His heart that nothing and no one else can fill. His love isn't conditional; it doesn't wait for us to be perfect or expect us to have everything figured out. Instead, His love meets us exactly where we are, with all our flaws, fears, and insecurities, and holds us with a tenderness that says, "You are mine, and I will never let you go." The Shepherd's voice of love is like a steady river that flows through our lives, bringing peace to our hearts, strength to our spirits, and comfort to our souls. This love doesn't come and go based on how we're doing or how we feel; it's an everlasting love, a love that stands strong through every season of life, through every joy and every sorrow. His voice of love calls us to rest, to trust, and to believe that we are worth loving, that we are worth knowing, and that we are worth keeping. The Shepherd's love fills us in ways that nothing else can, giving us a sense of belonging, purpose, and peace that is not dependent on our circumstances. It's a love that knows no limits, a love that reaches out to us in our highest moments and our lowest, lifting us up, encouraging us, and filling us with a hope that is as steady as it is gentle. His love is satisfying because it doesn't leave us longing for more; it meets every need, fills every gap, and reassures us that we are seen, understood, and valued. The Shepherd's voice of love doesn't change with time or fade with distance; it remains as strong and true today as it was yesterday and will be tomorrow. This everlasting love is like a foundation that holds us steady, a rock we can stand on, knowing that no matter what happens, we are safe, we are loved, and we are secure. His love is not just words; it's an action, a commitment, a promise that He will be with us always, loving us with a passion that never wavers and a grace that never ends. The Shepherd's love satisfies our deepest longings, the unspoken needs we carry, the dreams we hold close, and the fears we try to hide. His voice of love speaks directly to our hearts, filling us with a peace that says, "You are enough, just as you are, and you are deeply, unconditionally loved." In a world that often feels conditional, where love can seem fragile or hard to find, the Shepherd's love is a steady, reassuring presence, a love that doesn't turn away, doesn't grow tired, and doesn't give up on us. This is the kind of love that fills us up, that satisfies every longing, and that reminds us we are more than enough in His eyes. The Shepherd's love is like a shelter, a refuge, a place where we can come as we are, without fear of rejection or disappointment. His voice is a soothing balm, a gentle reminder that no matter where we've been or what we've done, we are welcomed, accepted, and treasured. His love is not about what we do but about who we are to Him—His beloved, His chosen, His cherished. When He says, "I have loved thee with an everlasting love," it's a promise that we are forever held in His embrace, that we are never outside the reach of His love, and that we are forever wanted. His love satisfies us because it gives us a sense of worth and belonging, a peace that nothing in this world can give or take away. It's a love that doesn't diminish with our doubts or disappear in our struggles; it's a love that grows with us, that walks beside us, and that holds us through every season of life. His voice of love calls us to believe in ourselves, to trust that we are worthy of this love, and to let go of any doubts or fears that try to tell us otherwise. The Shepherd's voice is a constant, a reassurance that even when we don't feel lovable, even when we struggle to see our own worth, He sees it, He knows it, and He celebrates it. His love is a gift, a treasure that fills us with a joy and a peace that is beyond anything the world can offer. This everlasting love is not just a feeling; it's a promise, a commitment, a truth that stands firm no matter what. When we feel lost, His love calls us home; when we feel broken, His love heals; and when we feel alone, His love reminds us that we are held close, always and forever. The Shepherd's love is a satisfying love, a love that fills us up and reminds us that we are never alone, never forgotten, and never unloved. So when we hear His voice say, "Yea, I have loved thee with an everlasting love," let it remind us that we are cherished, that we are valued, and that we are always held in the arms of a Shepherd whose love is forever, unchanging, and complete. His voice of love is our comfort, our peace, and our joy, a constant assurance that no matter where life takes us, we are forever loved, forever held, and forever His.

Chapter 27 - Securing Voice of Reassurance

The Shepherd's voice is a securing voice of reassurance, a voice that speaks right into our hearts with the kind of comfort and peace we all long for, saying, "Let not your heart be troubled: ye believe in God, believe also in me." This voice is like a gentle hand on our shoulder, calming the storms of worry, doubt, and fear that sometimes build up inside us. Imagine a voice that knows exactly how you're feeling, that sees the anxieties, the silent questions, and the moments of insecurity, and reaches out to say, "It's okay, you don't have to be afraid. I am here." This is the Shepherd's voice—steady, reassuring, and filled with a kindness that invites us to lay down our burdens, to let go of our anxious thoughts, and to find peace in His constant presence. His voice doesn't tell us to ignore our problems or pretend everything is fine; instead, it meets us in the middle of our troubles, acknowledging our concerns and offering a deep, lasting reassurance that everything will be okay because we're not facing life alone. The Shepherd's voice reminds us that we can believe in Him, that we can trust Him fully, because He is faithful, unchanging, and always near. His words are a promise, a foundation that we can stand on even when everything else feels shaky or uncertain. This voice of reassurance doesn't rely on empty phrases or distant promises; it's grounded in a love that is real, a presence that is close, and a commitment that never wavers. When we feel overwhelmed, His voice invites us to take a breath, to quiet our racing minds, and to remember that we are held in the hands of Someone who sees the whole picture, who knows exactly what we need, and who is fully capable of carrying us through whatever comes our way. His voice is like a lifeline, a safe place where we can bring all our fears, our doubts, and our questions, knowing that we will be met with patience, understanding, and a love that refuses to let us go. The Shepherd's reassurance is not just a comforting thought; it's a powerful truth that steadies our hearts, reminding us that we don't have to have all the answers or control everything because He is with us, guiding us, protecting us, and providing for us every step of the way. His voice of reassurance tells us that we can let go of our need to control, our habit of overthinking, and our fears of the unknown, and simply trust that He is working all things together for our good. Even when we don't see the full picture or understand the why behind every challenge, His voice assures us that He is right beside us, that He is the anchor in every storm, and that we are never left to navigate life alone. His presence brings a calm that the world can't offer, a peace that fills us even in the midst of life's uncertainties. When He says, "Let not your heart be troubled," He's inviting us to release our worries, to trust in His care, and to rest in the knowledge that we are safe in His hands. His voice of reassurance is a reminder that we are not walking this path by ourselves; we have a Shepherd who loves us deeply, who is invested in our well-being, and who is fully committed to seeing us through. His reassurance is gentle, patient, and kind, a constant source of peace that reminds us we don't have to be strong on our own. The Shepherd's voice doesn't demand that we be fearless or unbreakable; it simply invites us to lean on Him, to draw strength from His presence, and to believe that no matter what, we are loved, we are held, and we are safe. His voice is a steadying force, calming our anxious thoughts, filling us with hope, and helping us to believe that there is always a way forward, a reason to keep going, and a peace that is stronger than any fear. The Shepherd's voice of reassurance gives us the courage to face each day, each challenge, and each unknown, with a heart that is anchored in the knowledge that we are not alone. His voice calls us to let go of our fears, to trust in His unfailing love, and to believe that everything will be okay, even if we don't yet see how. His presence is our peace, our security, and our comfort, a constant reminder that we are forever held, forever loved, and forever reassured by the Shepherd who knows us, cares for us, and will never leave us alone. So when we hear His voice say, "Let not your heart be troubled," let it be a reminder that we are safe, we are loved, and we are always held in the unbreakable, all-encompassing embrace of the Shepherd who is with us, now and always. His voice of reassurance is our peace, our strength, and our hope, a constant assurance that we are never alone, that we are deeply loved, and that we are forever secure in His care.

Chapter 28 - Seeking Voice of Redemption

The Shepherd's voice is a seeking voice of redemption, a voice that reaches out to every part of us that feels lost, broken, or unworthy, saying with tender love, "The Son of man is come to seek and to save that which was lost." This isn't just a story or a statement; it's a promise, a mission, and a personal commitment from the One who sees us, knows us, and values us beyond measure. Imagine a love so deep and determined that it never stops reaching out, never stops searching, never gives up on us, no matter how far we've strayed or how hidden we feel. The Shepherd's voice calls to us, not with anger or disappointment, but with a heart full of mercy, compassion, and the relentless desire to bring us back to where we belong. His voice is like a gentle, steady hand reaching out in the darkness, a light that shines in the lonely places of our hearts, offering hope and healing. He knows every path we've taken, every mistake, every regret, and He doesn't turn away from any of it; instead, He steps right into our story, offering redemption and restoration. His voice of redemption tells us that we are not defined by our past, our failures, or our missteps; we are defined by His love, His grace, and His unchanging desire to bring us into the fullness of life. This voice of redemption is not distant or indifferent; it's a voice that actively seeks us, pursues us, and reminds us that we are not forgotten, that we are never too lost for His love to find. He searches for us like a shepherd searches for a lost sheep, not out of obligation but out of pure love, a love that values each of us uniquely and profoundly. His voice calls us to let go of shame, to release the guilt that weighs us down, and to trust that we are worthy of being found, worthy of being saved, and worthy of the new beginning He offers. The Shepherd's voice of redemption is patient and kind, understanding that sometimes we resist, sometimes we hide, sometimes we feel too far gone—but He never stops calling, never stops reaching out, and never loses hope for us. His voice assures us that there is no place too dark, no sin too great, and no distance too far for His love to reach. When He says He came "to seek and to save that which was lost," it means He values each of us so much that He would move heaven and earth to bring us back. He doesn't come to judge or to condemn; He comes to lift us up, to restore our dignity, and to give us a sense of purpose and belonging. His seeking voice of redemption reminds us that we are seen, we are known, and we are deeply, unconditionally loved, just as we are. This voice doesn't ignore our struggles or minimize our pain; it acknowledges every part of our journey, meeting us with understanding and compassion, and offering a way forward. His voice of redemption is like a song of hope that plays softly in the background of our lives, calling us to believe in the possibility of change, healing, and growth. The Shepherd doesn't force us to come; He invites us, patiently waiting, gently guiding, and continually offering His love. His redemption is not about erasing who we are; it's about bringing out the best in us, about restoring what was broken, and helping us to see ourselves through His loving eyes. His voice calls us to rise above our past, to step out of the shadows, and to embrace the new life He offers—a life filled with grace, peace, and the joy of being fully accepted. The Shepherd's seeking voice tells us that we don't have to be perfect to be loved; we are loved right here, right now, as we are, with all our flaws, fears, and imperfections. His redemption is a gift, a second chance, a new beginning that assures us we are never too lost to be found. He doesn't keep a record of our wrongs or hold our mistakes over us; instead, He wipes the slate clean, offering forgiveness that is complete, healing that is deep, and love that is everlasting. His voice of redemption invites us to lay down our burdens, to surrender our doubts, and to let go of the things that hold us back, trusting that He is ready and willing to help us start fresh. The Shepherd's voice of redemption is a constant, a faithful reminder that we are not alone, that we are never abandoned, and that we are held in a love that seeks us, finds us, and brings us home. His voice tells us that we are not defined by where we've been or what we've done; we are defined by His love, His grace, and His promise that we belong to Him. So when we hear His voice, calling us with love, saying, "I have come to seek and to save that which was lost," let it remind us that we are wanted, that we are cherished, and that we have a place in His heart forever. His seeking voice of redemption is our hope, our strength, and our peace, a constant assurance that we are never beyond His reach, never outside His love, and always, always held in His everlasting embrace.

Chapter 29 - Sincere Voice of Truth

The Shepherd's voice is a sincere voice of truth, a voice that speaks with unwavering honesty and deep love, declaring, "I am the way, the truth, and the life." These words are not only a statement but a promise, an invitation, and a guide that reaches into the very heart of our lives, offering a path that is grounded in truth, filled with hope, and marked by a love that wants only the best for us. Imagine a voice that always tells you what is real, what matters most, and what you need to hear, even when life feels confusing or overwhelming. This is the voice of the Shepherd—a voice that doesn't just tell us what we want to hear but offers the truth we need, gently guiding us, supporting us, and encouraging us to walk a path that brings real joy, peace, and purpose. His voice doesn't waver with popular opinion or shift based on trends; it is a steady and reliable anchor that keeps us grounded in what is true, even when the world around us is constantly changing. This sincere voice of truth calls us to look beyond the superficial, to dig deeper, and to build our lives on a foundation that is solid and unshakeable. The Shepherd doesn't just point out the truth; He embodies it, showing us through His actions, His love, and His promises what it truly means to live with integrity, compassion, and courage. His voice tells us that we don't have to be perfect, that we don't have to pretend or hide, because the truth is that we are loved just as we are, deeply and unconditionally. His words invite us to find our true selves in Him, to let go of any masks or fears, and to embrace a life that is free, honest, and rooted in His love. This voice of truth doesn't condemn or criticize; it uplifts, it heals, and it sets us on a path where we can be fully ourselves, knowing that we are seen, known, and valued. The Shepherd's voice is a light in the darkness, a compass when we feel lost, and a friend who walks with us every step of the way, reminding us that we are never alone. His sincerity gives us confidence, helping us to trust that no matter what, He is with us, guiding us, and showing us the way. This voice of truth offers clarity in the midst of confusion, peace in the midst of fear, and hope in the midst of doubt. The Shepherd's truth is not just a set of rules or ideas; it's a way of life that leads to joy, fulfillment, and lasting happiness. His voice calls us to live authentically, to embrace who we are, and to walk a path that reflects the love and truth He has shown us. When He says, "I am the way, the truth, and the life," He's reminding us that we don't have to find our way alone; He is here to lead us, to teach us, and to help us discover the true purpose and meaning of our lives. His voice reassures us that we are not a mistake, that we are not lost causes, and that we have a beautiful purpose that He is ready to help us fulfill. The Shepherd's voice is one of love and grace, a voice that never gives up on us, never turns away, and never stops guiding us toward the life we were meant to live. His truth is a gift, a treasure that brings peace to our hearts, clarity to our minds, and courage to our spirits. This voice doesn't change with circumstances or fade over time; it is a constant presence, a steady hand that holds us close, and a gentle reminder that we are loved beyond measure. The Shepherd's voice of truth is a safe place, a refuge where we can find rest, hope, and encouragement, knowing that we are always accepted, always valued, and always loved. His words are a promise that we are never alone, that we are always seen, and that we are held by a love that is pure, sincere, and forever true.

Chapter 30 - Saving Voice of Deliverance

The Shepherd's voice is a saving voice of deliverance, a voice that reaches out to us in our most difficult, fearful, and overwhelming moments, saying, "Call upon me in the day of trouble: I will deliver thee." This voice isn't just offering temporary comfort or words to get us by—it's making a promise, a commitment that no matter what we face, we are not alone and we have a lifeline that is always there, waiting for us to reach out. Imagine a love so strong, so present, that it is ready to step into any darkness, any struggle, any fear, and bring us safely through it, lifting us out of despair and placing our feet back on solid ground. This is the Shepherd's deliverance—a saving grace that doesn't judge us for being afraid or lost, but instead, calls us to lean on Him, to trust that there is no trouble too big, no problem too complicated, and no fear too great for His power to overcome. His voice is like a constant presence, a hand reaching through the chaos, ready to hold us, guide us, and bring us peace. He doesn't wait for us to be perfect or brave enough on our own; He simply waits for us to call on Him, knowing that we are human, that we have limits, and that sometimes life feels like too much to bear alone. The Shepherd's voice of deliverance isn't harsh or distant—it's filled with compassion, understanding the depths of our pain and struggles, and offering a refuge, a safe place to let go and let Him take over. His promise to deliver us isn't just about pulling us out of our troubles; it's about walking with us through them, giving us the strength we didn't know we had, and reassuring us that, no matter how dark or confusing things seem, He has a plan and a way out. His voice doesn't condemn us for feeling weak or afraid; instead, it reminds us that even in our most vulnerable moments, we are loved, we are valued, and we are never abandoned. The Shepherd's deliverance is like a steady hand on our shoulder, a whisper of hope in the storm, reminding us that we don't have to figure everything out on our own because He is with us, guiding us and protecting us every step of the way. When we call on Him, it's like a door opens, letting His peace, His power, and His love flood into our hearts, filling us with the courage to keep going, the faith to believe in better days, and the assurance that we are never fighting our battles alone. His voice of deliverance doesn't just lift us out of our troubles; it teaches us, strengthens us, and helps us see the beauty and strength that He's placed within us. He doesn't simply solve our problems for us; He walks with us through them, helping us to grow, to trust, and to find joy even in the midst of difficulty. The Shepherd's deliverance is not a quick fix; it's a transformation, a journey of healing, and a pathway to peace that comes from knowing that we are loved deeply, protected fiercely, and held tenderly by the One who knows us best. His voice calls us to release our fears, to cast our anxieties on Him, and to rest in the knowledge that His love is greater than any challenge, any hurt, and any fear we face. His deliverance is a promise that we are never alone, that we are always seen, and that we are forever safe in His care. When He says, "I will deliver thee," He is offering us a gift, a lifeline, and a hope that cannot be shaken. This isn't just a promise for when times are easy or when we're feeling strong; it's a promise for our darkest days, our hardest nights, and our deepest struggles. His voice of deliverance is a constant reminder that we are precious, that we are worth saving, and that we are loved beyond measure. He doesn't see us as problems to be fixed or burdens to be carried; He sees us as His beloved, His cherished, and His own, and He will go to any lengths to bring us out of the shadows and into His light. The Shepherd's deliverance is more than a rescue   it's a renewal, a second chance, and a new beginning, helping us to let go of our past, to rise above our fears, and to live with the confidence that we are forever held in His hands. His voice tells us that we don't have to be afraid of the future or haunted by our past because His love covers all, heals all, and renews all. His deliverance is a beacon of hope, a reminder that no matter what we face, we have a Savior who will always come for us, who will always fight for us, and who will never, ever let us go. So when we hear His voice, calling us to trust, to call on Him, and to believe in His promise, let it remind us that we are safe, we are loved, and we are forever secure in the saving grace of the Shepherd who will deliver us, now and always. His voice of deliverance is our refuge, our strength, and our peace, a constant reminder that we are held, that we are valued, and that we are forever safe in His loving embrace.

Chapter 31 - Shout of Victory

The Shepherd's voice is a mighty shout of victory, a voice that echoes with strength, joy, and unbreakable hope, proclaiming, "Thanks be to God, which giveth us the victory through our Lord Jesus Christ." This isn't just a statement—it's a declaration of triumph, a resounding promise that no matter what challenges we face, no matter the obstacles that rise before us, we are not only survivors but conquerors through His love and power. Imagine a love so powerful, a strength so enduring, that it can overcome anything, even the darkest night, the hardest battle, or the deepest sorrow. This victory isn't something we earn or achieve by our own efforts; it's a gift, a victory given to us by the One who loves us beyond measure and fought the ultimate battle for us. The Shepherd's shout of victory is like a battle cry that fills our hearts with courage, reminding us that we are not defeated, that we are not overcome, because He has already secured the victory on our behalf. His voice lifts us up, giving us the confidence to stand tall, to walk forward with strength and peace, knowing that nothing can separate us from His love and that no challenge is too great for Him. His victory is our assurance that we don't have to be perfect, that we don't have to carry every burden alone, because He has already overcome every struggle, every sin, and every fear. This voice of victory is a beacon of hope, a promise that whatever we face, there is a way through, a path to freedom, and a hope that will never fade. The Shepherd doesn't just shout this victory from afar; He walks with us in every step, every trial, and every moment of doubt, reminding us that His strength is made perfect in our weakness, that His love fills every gap, and that His victory is as real and true today as it was on the day He won it. His shout of victory isn't just for moments of celebration; it's there for us in our quiet struggles, in our hardest nights, and in the times we feel most defeated. This shout of victory fills us with the strength to keep going, to rise again, and to believe that we are not defined by our failures but by His unbreakable love. His voice doesn't ignore our pain or pretend that life is always easy; it acknowledges our struggles, stands with us in our battles, and reminds us that through Him, we have a power and a hope that can never be taken away. His victory is a victory over every fear, every doubt, and every challenge that comes our way, filling us with a joy and peace that stand strong, no matter what. The Shepherd's victory tells us that we are not alone in our battles, that we are not forgotten in our struggles, and that we are held by a love that conquered even death itself. His voice of victory is a reminder that no matter how many times we fall, we can always get back up, because His strength is with us, His love empowers us, and His victory is ours to claim. This victory isn't just about winning battles; it's about finding peace in knowing that we are loved, we are valued, and we are forever held in the hands of the One who conquered it all for us. The Shepherd's victory fills us with a sense of purpose, a joy that is unshakeable, and a hope that lights up even the darkest of days. His shout of victory tells us that we are more than conquerors, that we are children of a God who delights in us, who celebrates us, and who walks with us through every season of life. His victory is our strength, our peace, and our reason to keep going, to keep hoping, and to keep believing that no matter what, we are safe, we are loved, and we are forever victorious in Him. So when we hear His shout of victory, let it remind us that we are never alone, that we are cherished beyond measure, and that we are forever victorious through the love and grace of our Shepherd. His shout of victory is our anthem, our song, and our promise that we are forever held, forever loved, and forever victorious in His embrace.

Conclusion

As we come to the end of "The Shepherd's Voice", it's clear that His voice is not just one sound or message but a whole symphony of love, guidance, comfort, strength, and hope, a presence that meets us in every moment of our lives. The Shepherd's voice is gentle yet strong, comforting yet powerful, reaching us wherever we are and speaking into the depths of our hearts with a love that is constant and true. Through every struggle, every joy, every moment of doubt or fear, His voice is there, calling us by name, reminding us that we are never alone. His words are filled with grace, speaking to us with a kindness that reassures and heals, a promise that stays steady when life feels shaky. His voice is the anchor that holds us, the light that guides us, and the strength that lifts us, reminding us that we are precious, beloved, and worth every ounce of His love. In a world that can feel so uncertain, His voice is the one thing we can always count on, a voice that is unwavering, patient, and endlessly compassionate. He doesn't just speak to the parts of us that are strong or sure; He speaks to the broken, the uncertain, the weary, and the searching, reaching every corner of our hearts with a gentleness that restores and renews. The Shepherd's voice offers more than just words; it offers us a relationship, an invitation to walk through life with the One who knows us best and loves us most. When we feel lost, His voice calls us back; when we feel burdened, His voice says, "Come to Me," and when we feel afraid, His voice assures us that we are safe in His care. This voice is always near, always ready to comfort, to guide, and to give us the peace and strength we need to face whatever comes our way. It's a voice that says we are loved beyond measure, that we are not defined by our mistakes, and that we have a purpose that is beautiful and meaningful. As we go forward, let's remember the many ways the Shepherd's voice speaks into our lives, inviting us to trust, to hope, to love, and to rest in the knowledge that we are His. Let's carry His words in our hearts, knowing that whatever life brings, His voice will always be there to guide us, comfort us, and remind us that we are never alone. "The Shepherd's Voice" is a voice we can return to again and again, a voice that reminds us of who we are and whose we are, a voice that loves us, lifts us, and leads us every step of the way.

Don't miss out!

Visit the website below and you can sign up to receive emails whenever Joshua Rhoades publishes a new book. There's no charge and no obligation.

https://books2read.com/r/B-A-AJLBB-QPAEF

BOOKS2READ

Connecting independent readers to independent writers.

Did you love *The Shepherd's Voice*? Then you should read *Renewed Hope- How to Find Encouragement in God*[1] by Joshua Rhoades!

[2]

In a world where challenges and hardships seem to come at us from every side, it's easy to feel overwhelmed, discouraged, and even hopeless. We all face moments when we wonder how we will ever make it through the difficulties we encounter. But in these times, the Bible offers us a powerful example of finding strength and hope, no matter the circumstances. In 1 Samuel 30:6, we read about David, a man who faced great trials and overwhelming odds, yet in the midst of it all, "David encouraged himself in the LORD his God." This simple yet profound statement serves as the foundation for this book, "Renewed Hope- How to Find Encouragement in God." David's life was filled with ups and downs, moments of triumph and times of deep despair. He knew what it was like to be pursued by enemies, to experience loss, and to feel abandoned. Yet, even in his darkest hours, David found a way to renew his hope by turning to God. He didn't rely on his own strength or seek comfort in worldly solutions. Instead, he looked to the LORD, drawing strength and encouragement from his relationship with God. This book is an invitation to explore how we, too, can find renewed hope and encouragement in God, just as David did. It is a guide to understanding the power of faith, prayer, and trusting in God's promises, even when life seems unbearable. Throughout these pages, we will explore practical ways to draw closer to God, to encourage ourselves

---

1. https://books2read.com/u/boeko1

2. https://books2read.com/u/boeko1

in Him, and to discover the peace and strength that come from relying on the LORD. Whether you are facing a specific challenge right now or simply want to deepen your relationship with God, this book will provide you with the tools and inspiration you need to find encouragement in the LORD. As we journey together through the principles found in David's example, you will learn how to shift your focus from the problems that surround you to the God who sustains you. You will discover that no matter what life throws at you, there is always hope in the LORD, and by encouraging yourself in Him, you can face any situation with renewed strength and confidence. This is not just a book about surviving difficult times, but about thriving through them by finding your hope and encouragement in the unchanging character of God. So, whether you are struggling with personal challenges, feeling weighed down by the burdens of life, or simply seeking a deeper sense of peace and purpose, "Renewed Hope-How to Find Encouragement in God" is here to remind you that you are not alone, and that with God, there is always a reason to hope. Let David's example inspire you to turn to the LORD, to find your strength in Him, and to walk forward with a renewed sense of hope, no matter what you face.

www.ingramcontent.com/pod-product-compliance
Lightning Source LLC
Chambersburg PA
CBHW051904130726
47987CB00002B/976